CAESURA IN CRYPTOGRAPHY:
MY FIRST WORKSHOP ABOUT ENCRYPTION

An Introduction with Teaching and Learning Material for School, University and Leisure.

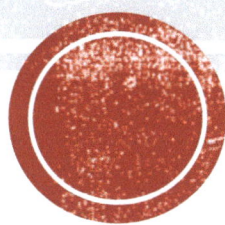

Available as:
• PDF-E-Book (colored, ISBN: 9783752676921)
• Paperback Booklet (PB 9783751989497)
• Colored Hardcover (HC 9783751989527)

Evelyn Ackermann & Michael Klein

Impressum:

Ackermann, Evelyn & Klein, Michael:
  Caesura in Cryptography: My first Workshop about Encryption
  - An Introduction with Teaching and Learning Material for School, University and Leisure.
  © 2020. (HC Colored ISBN 9783751989527) (PB Grey ISBN 9783751989497) (PDF Colored ISBN 9783752676921).

Manufacturer / Publisher / Printing:
BoD, Norderstedt - http://www.bod.de
More bibliographic info under: https://portal.dnb.de

CONTENT: WHAT 🔍

1. What, Why & How of Encryption.
2. Personal Motivation to be engaged within Cryptography.
3. Asymmetric & Symmetric Encryption.
4. Third Epoch of Cryptography: No Key Transport – instead: Derived Keys.
5. Caesura in Cryptography: Juggernaut and Secret Stream Keys.
6. Ciphers & Algorithms & Multi-Encryption: e.g. McEliece & NTRU.
7. Else to know: RNG, MAC, OTP, GNUPG, PKI, Hash, Signatures, GoldBugs, EPKS, SMP.
8. End-to-End Encryption: Instant Perfect Forward Secrecy (IPFS).
9. Cryptographic Calling: e.g. Two-Way-Calling, Repleo, EPKS, AutoCrypt.
10. Volatile Encryption & Exponential Encryption.
11. Cryptographic Discovery & Cryptographic Tokens.
12. Echo Protocol & Graph Theory.
13. POPTASTIC Protocol: Chat over POP3/IMAP.
14. Spot-On Encryption Suite as elaborated Software for Learning & Tutorials.
15. Quantum Computing and Cryptography.
16. Frameworks & Libraries: e.g. McNoodle McEliece library (C++).
17. Tools: POPTASTIC Delta Chat, Smoke McEliece Java Messenger, et al..
18. Trends on Crypto Messaging & Open Source Cryptography.
19. Encryption of the Hard Disc, Text and Files, P2P Networks.
20. Trusted Execution Environments (TEE) & SAM Architecture .
21. National Sovereignty of cryptographic projects and open source worldwide contributions.
22. Your Evaluation & further Bibliography.

Ackermann & Klein: Caesura in Cryptography (2020)

WHY IS ENCRYPTION A STANDARD?

- **Economy is based on encryption**. Companies, people, developers and providers of innovation need digital security.

- **Defending critical infrastructure**: Providers of essential services, such as banking, health, electricity, water, Internet and other critical infrastructure providers, are to be empowered to provide the best available encryption and security technologies.

- **Guaranteeing data security - Law and regulations** require encryption: E.g. Healthcare providers are required by the Health Insurance Portability and Accountability Act (HIPAA) to implement security. Providers of data services - storing, managing or transmitting personal or business data - must guarantee to use the best available technology to thwart attacks. In Europe GPDR/DSGVO law requires the protection of sensitive or personal data.

- **Privacy by Default**: Individuals have **human rights to be secure** in their public, private and commercial lives and interactions.

- National, state and local agencies should ensure that the **governmental data & information** they hold is protected.

- All **internet traffic is permanently recorded** as the Snowden papers reveal (since 2013). Send only Ciphertext to the Internet.

- Hacking and **collecting user data** is today big business.

- **Old Internet protocols** provide only plain text and require a replacement: e.g. #NEWIP, E-Mail-Institutions & IMAP & Ozone Post Boxes, Echo Protocol replacing TCP Protocol.

Ackermann & Klein: Caesura in Cryptography (2020)

UNDERSTANDING CRYPTOGRAPHY: WHAT, WHY & HOW

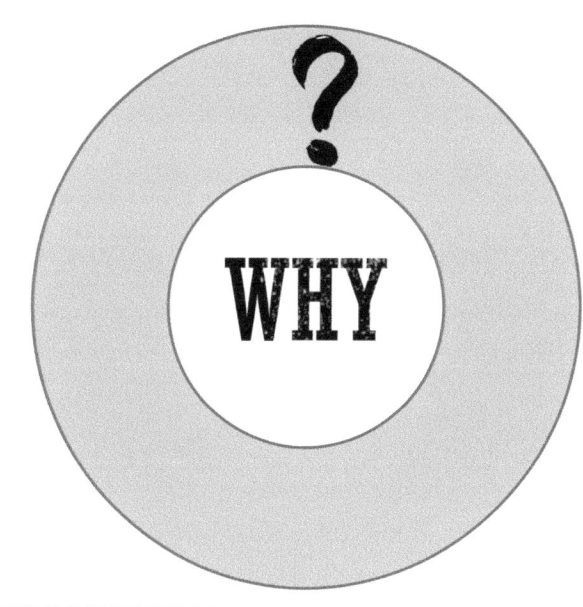

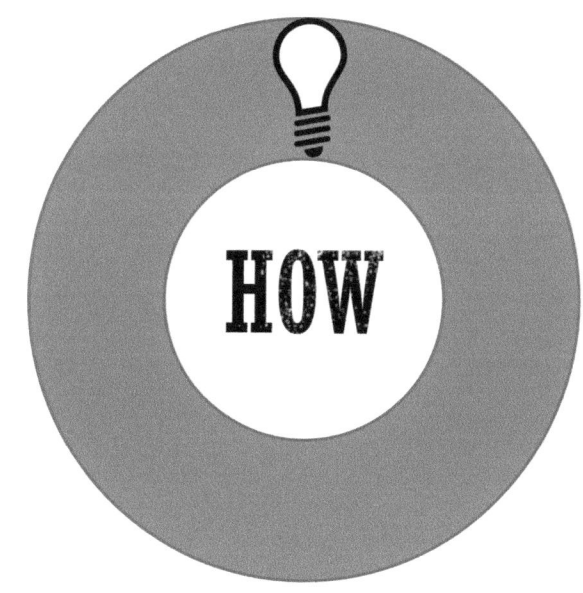

WHAT ARE WE LEARNING?
- Having an overview,
- Encrypting chat messages,
- Encrypting e-mails,
- Encrypting files,
- Using secure passwords,
- How to clean cookies,
- Browse anonymously,
- Test and compare tools,
- Be arware of risks.

WHY IS ENCRYPTION IMPORTANT?
- Economy,
- Security,
- Law & Regulations,
- Privacy by Default,
- Human Rights,
- Governmental Data,
- Hacking is bug busines,
- Permanent Record of Net-Data,
- Old Plaintext Protocols.

HOW DO WE APPLY ENCRYPTION?
- Listening, being aware of the topic,
- Reading and learning,
- Understanding the Why,
- Knowing the terms & nomenclatura,
- Testing and using different tools,
- Interaction, networking, participation & speaking out,
- Being trained in the How,
- Writing manuals & policies,
- Learning to develop a client.

EXPECTATIONS

? WHAT'S YOUR STORY

- Learning the basics.
- Testing a tool.
- Compare software.
- Strengthen open source applications with encryption.
- Write an encrypted message to a friend.
- Build a new culture for encryption.
- Accelerate personal learnings in cryptography.
- Find friends to create a network for testing encrypted communication software.
- Find reasons why our organization should use cryptography.
- Find a deepend topic for my home work.
- Want to help a mobile & open source encryption application to improve.
- Need at work to message confidentially with clients, lawyers and informants.
- Share Experiences. Give us your feedback about to be deepend topics…

SOME GOALS FOR THIS INTRODUCTION COURSE

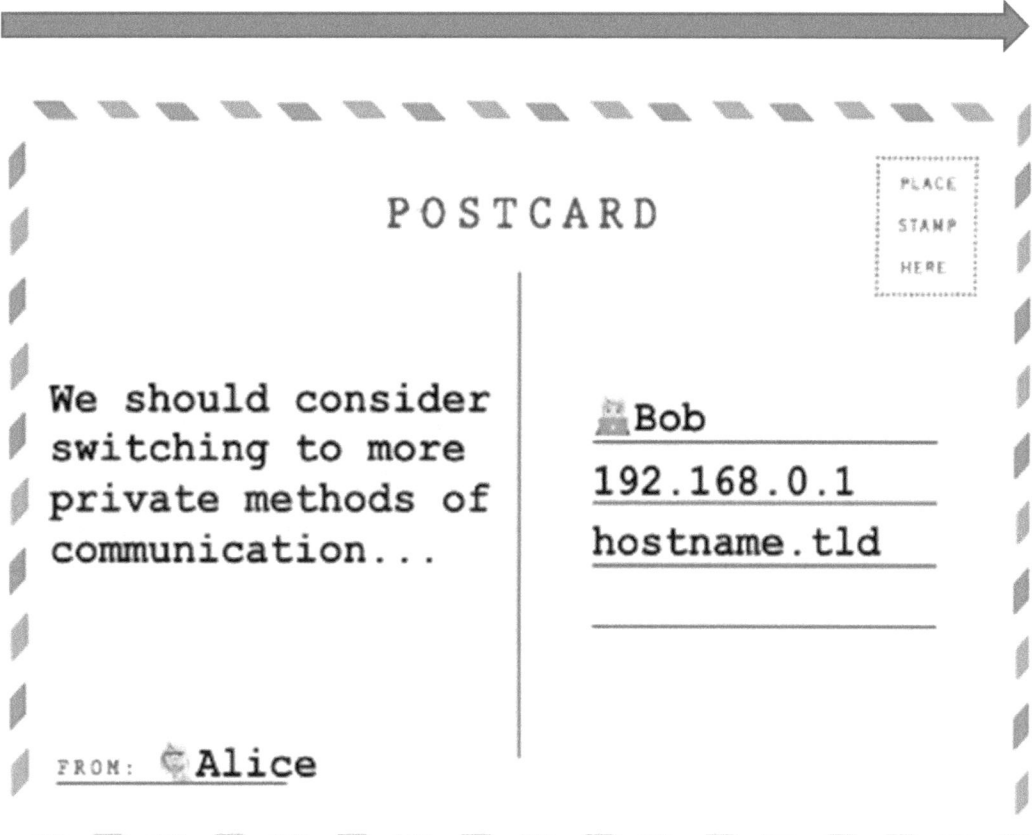

- Generating a key (pair).
- Set up your e-mail program to send and receive signed and encrypted e-mail.
- Set up your chat program to send and receive signed and encrypted chats.
- Send me an encrypted message.
- Knowing relevant terms & processes.
- Learn more about modern cryptographical methods.

EXERCISE: LET'S DO IT (IN A TEAM)

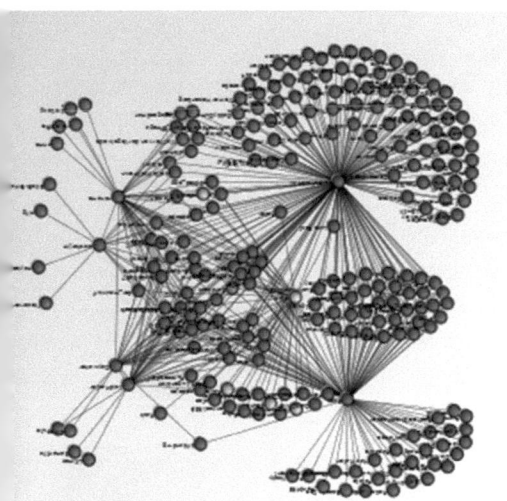

- Organize yourself: Devide your class into 5 subgroups.
- Everyone gets a printed copy / booklet of these slides.
- Every group gets ~15 slides assigned.
- All slides per group should be considered in a presentation.
- Present as group your assigend slides in a plenary session of 30 minutes. Consider another 20 minutes for discussion, questions and answers.
- For the next session prepare a practical exercise within the plenum in regard of your content (Part B of the session, 30 minutes).
- The next session starts with the presentation of the next group (Part A of the session). Then practical exercise of the last group.

If all presentations & practical exercises are done:

- Decide on which topic you personally want to investigate further!

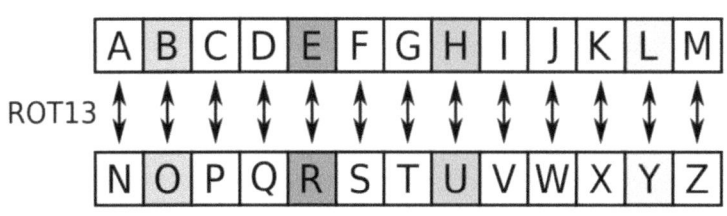

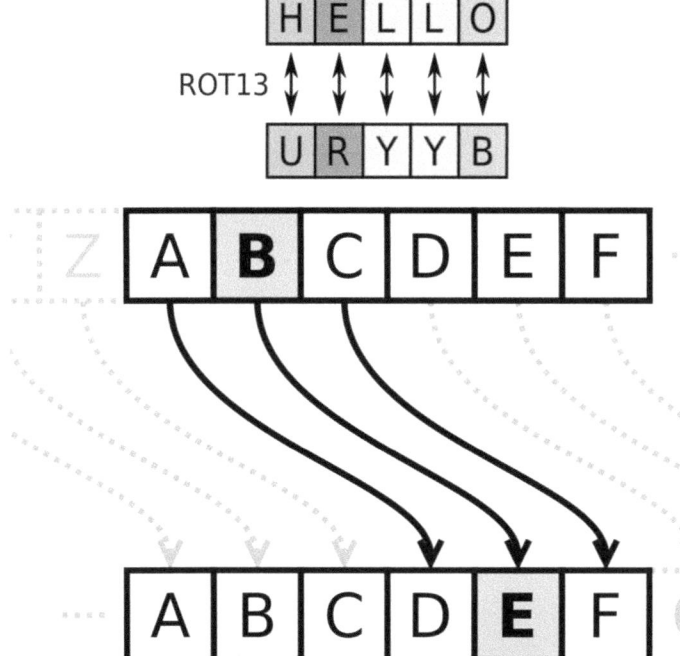

HISTORICAL METHODS OF CRYPTOGRAPHY

- A **Caesar's cipher** is a type of **substitution** cipher in which each letter in the plaintext is replaced by a letter some fixed number of positions down the alphabet. For example, with a right shift of 3: A would be replaced by D. The method is named after Julius Caesar, who used it in his private correspondence.

- Another application is the **ROT13** system, which replaces each letter by its partner 13 characters further along the alphabet. HELLO becomes URYYB.

- It is easily broken and offers in practice essentially no communications security.

SYMMETRIC & ASYMMETRIC ENCRYPTION

Symmetric Encryption

Also called: Gemini (Greek for Twins)

Examples: AES-256 / One-Time-Pad

1. Alice and Bob agree on a cryptosystem.
2. Alice and Bob agree on a key.
3. Alice takes her plaintext message and encrypts it using the encryption algorithm and the key. This creates a ciphertext message.
4. Alice sends the ciphertext message to Bob.
5. Bob decrypts the ciphertext message with the same algorithm and key and reads it.

Alice => same key => Bob

Key Transfer Problem,
if not Zero-Knowledge-Methods applied:
No key transfer with: Secret Stream Keys & Juggerknot Keys

Asymmetric Encryption

Also called: Public Key Infrastructure (PKI)

Examples: McEliece / NTRU Algorithms

1. Alice and Bob agree on a public-key cryptosystem, e.g. with McEliece algorithm.
2. Bob sends Alice his public key.
3. Alice encrypts her message using Bob's public key and sends it to Bob.
4. Bob decrypts Alice's message using his private key.

Alice:		Bob:
Public Key	$\xleftarrow{\text{exchange}}\rightarrow$	Public Key
Private Key		Private Key

Ackermann & Klein: Caesura in Cryptography (2020)

ASYMMETRIC ENCRYPTION IN DETAIL

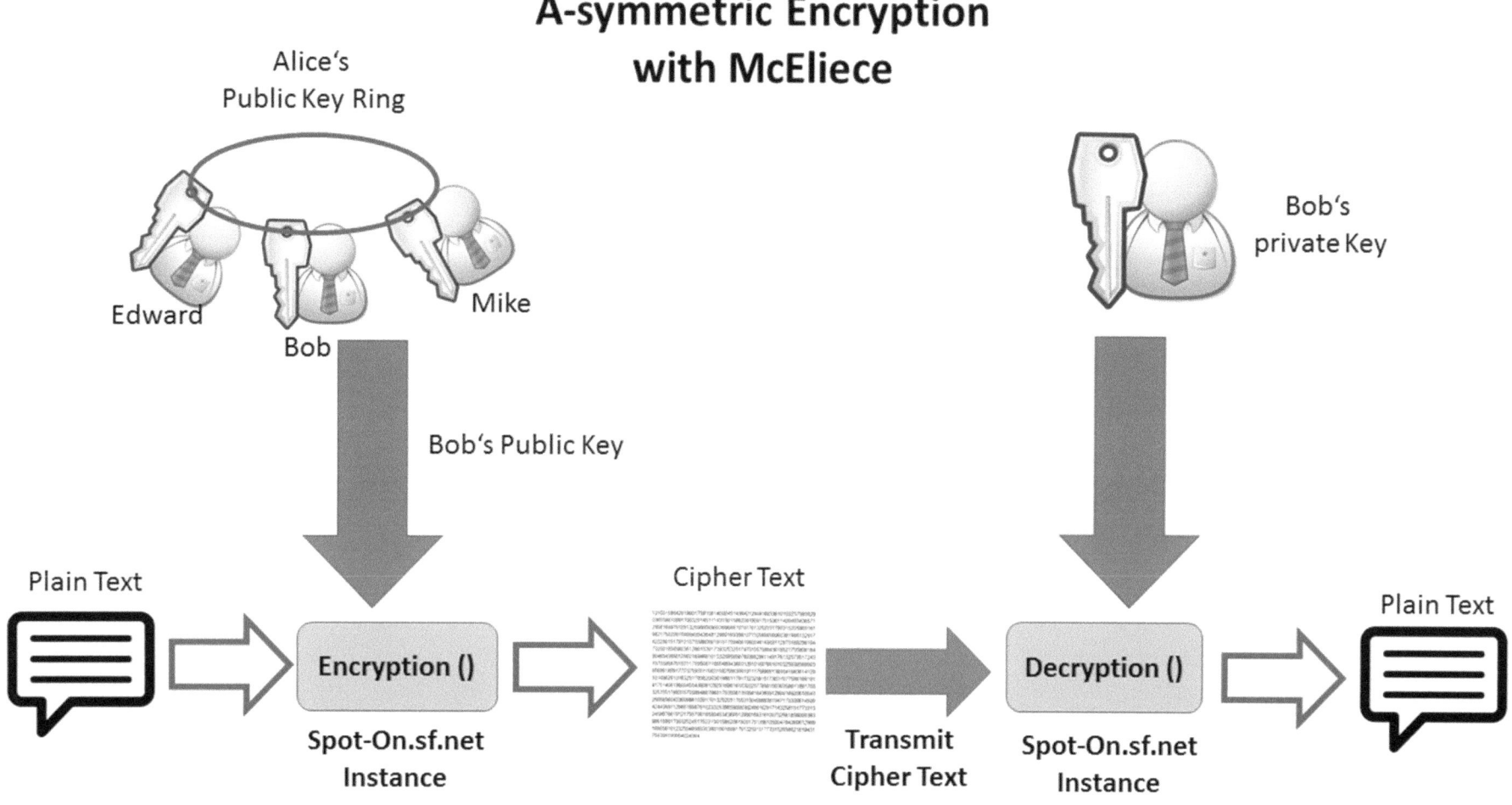

A-symmetric Encryption with McEliece

Alice's Public Key Ring

Edward
Bob
Mike

Bob's Public Key

Bob's private Key

Plain Text

Encryption ()
Spot-On.sf.net Instance

Cipher Text

Transmit Cipher Text

Decryption ()
Spot-On.sf.net Instance

Plain Text

*) Spot-On is a highly elaborated encryption suite software mostly used at university training lessons to study and learn encryption processes.

SYMMETRIC ENCRYPTION IN DETAIL

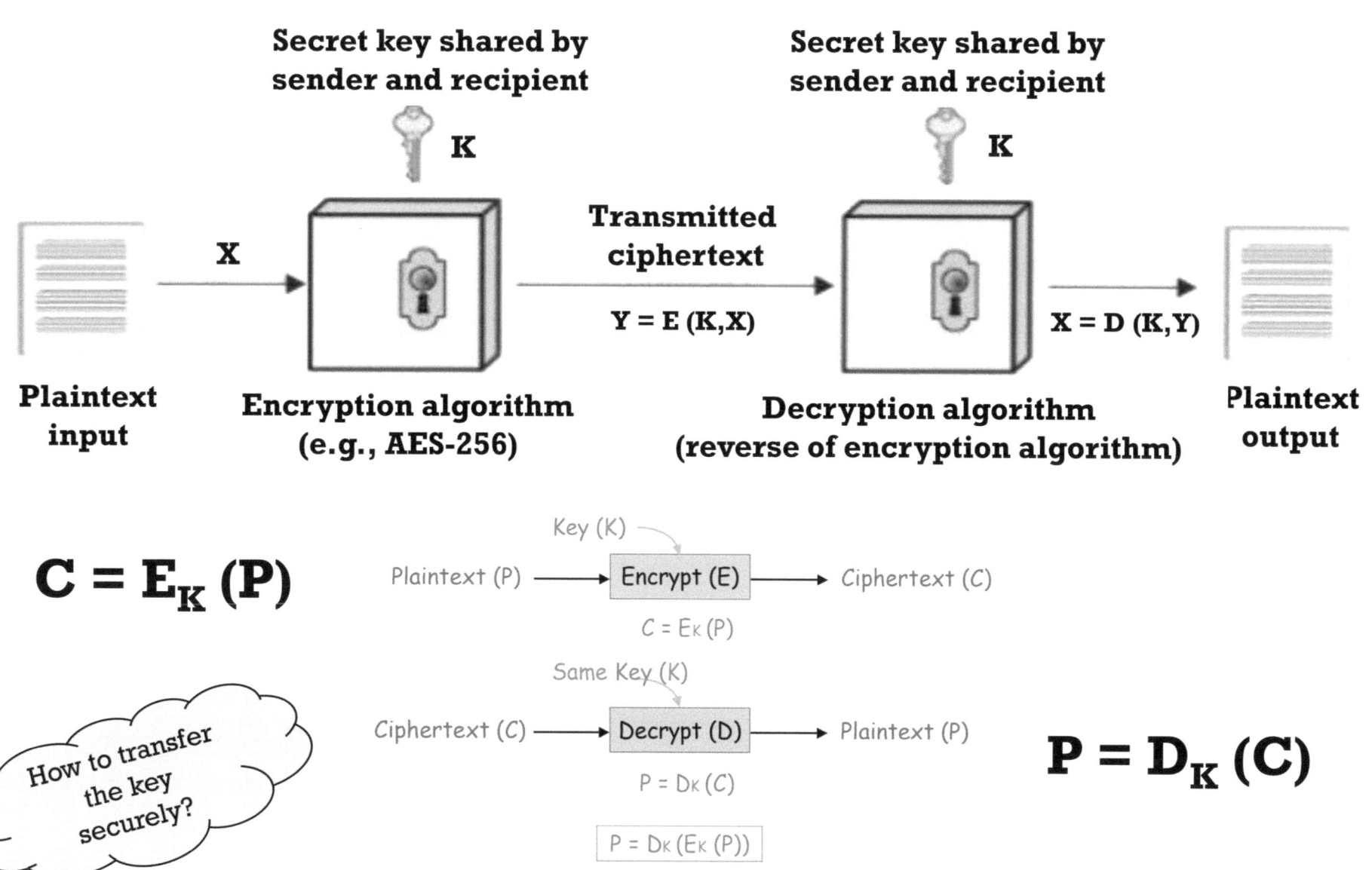

$$C = E_K (P)$$

$$P = D_K (C)$$

How to transfer the key securely?

Ackermann & Klein: Caesura in Cryptography (2020)

11

THIRD EPOCH OF CRYPTOGRAPHY: SOLVING THE KEY TRANSPORT PROBLEM?!

- Zero-Knowledge-Methods provide a key derivation without key transfer:

- E.g. Secret Key Streams.

- E.g. Juggerknot Keys.

- These keys are derived and not transferred.

- Definition of a new, the third ceasura in cryptography.

- Geminis / symmetric keys need not to be transferred anymore.

Peggy and Victor in the Ali Baba Cave:
(A) Peggy randomly takes either path A or B, while Victor waits outside.
(B) Victor chooses an exit path.
(C) Peggy reliably appears at the exit Victor names.

The Ali Baba Cave is a well-known story presenting the fundamental ideas of zero-knowledge proofs, first published by Jean-Jacques Quisquater and others in their paper "How to Explain Zero-Knowledge Protocols to Your Children".

Ackermann & Klein: Caesura in Cryptography (2020)

CAESURA IN CRYPTOGRAPHY: SECRET STREAMS

- Secret Streams denote the creation of numerous temporary keys, that are in the build process derived from a not-over-the-network transmitted passphrase. The keys come or are derived out of a Socialist Millionaire Process (SMP).

- In this process, both friends enter a secret password in their client - and this is not transmitted over the Internet. Using a mathematical method, a zero-knowledge proof, it is determined whether the same password has been entered on both sides.

- The so-called Socialist Millionaire Protocol produces the mathematical calculation of this Zero-Knowledge Proof.

- If the mathematical SMP proof is successful, it can be assumed that both communication participants have entered the same password into the mathematical process in each of their clients - without, however, that this password has ever been transmitted over the Internet.

- Secret Streams are programmed in C ++ and were first developed in the popular and above mentioned Encryption Suite Spot-On.

Ackermann & Klein: Caesura in Cryptography (2020)

13

CAESURA IN CRYPTOGRAPHY: JUGGERNKNOT KEYS

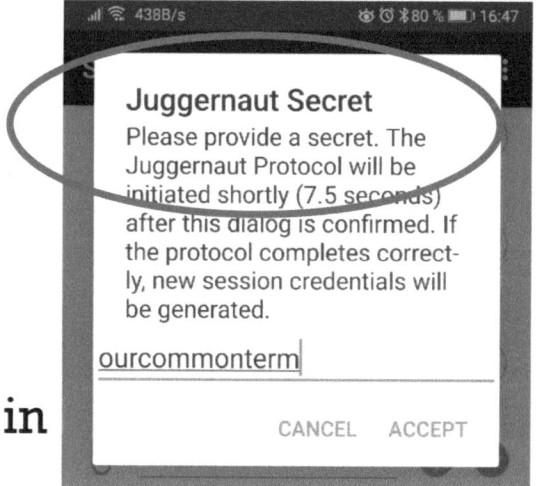

- An elimination of the key transport problem is also found in Juggerknot Keys.

- These are exemplary programmed in Java (in the application of the Crypto Chat Messenger Smoke for the Android operating system) and build on a similar method of a Zero-Knowledge Proof: With the difference that here not a (Socialist-Millionaire) SMP process was used, but the mathematically-similar process of the

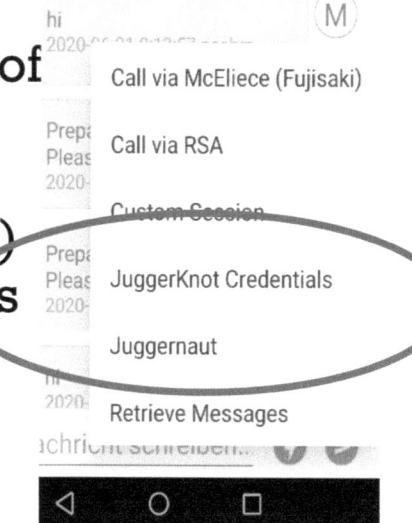

- Juggernaut PAKE Protocols, in which both communication partners - each on the own side - also enter a secret phrase, which in turn is not shared over the Internet.

- Then, temporary end-to-end encrypting keys are derived.

- Now one might want to consider that one has to exchange a secret before using the online Internet infrastructure, so this is only partially correct, because it is about picking up a keyword from a common pool of experience, without naming this keyword. Ultimately, in the simple case, each communication partner is indexed or mapped only once with an alias, and encryption can take place without the transfer of keys over the Internet.

TWO TYPES OF SYMMETRIC CIPHERS

In cryptography, a cipher is an algorithm for performing encryption or decryption - a series of well-defined steps that can be followed as a procedure. An alternative, less common term is encipherment. To encipher or encode is to convert information into cipher or code. In common parlance, "cipher" is synonymous with "code", as they are both a set of steps that encrypt a message.

Stream Cipher:

A stream cipher is a symmetric key cipher where plaintext digits are combined with a pseudorandom cipher digit stream (keystream). In a stream cipher, each plaintext digit is encrypted one at a time with the corresponding digit of the keystream, to give a digit of the ciphertext stream.

- **Encrypts one bit at a time.**
- Loose inspiration from the one-time pad.
- ChaCha is becoming the most widely used stream cipher in software; others are: RC4, A5/1, A5/2, Chameleon, FISH, Helix, ISAAC, MUGI, Panama, Phelix, Pike, Salsa20, SEAL, SOBER, SOBER-128, or WAKE.

Block Cipher:

A block cipher is a deterministic algorithm operating on fixed-length groups of bits, called blocks. It uses an unvarying transformation, that is, it uses a symmetric key. Even a secure block cipher is suitable only for the encryption of a single block of data at a time, using a fixed key.

- **Encrypts a block of bits at a time.**
- E.g. AES-256 (Advanced Encryption Standard).

ATTENDEES WANT MORE
PRACTICAL EXERCISES:

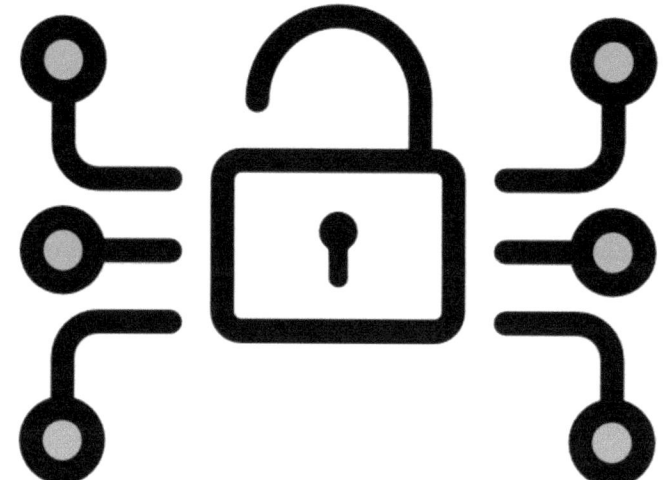

- Let´s create an asymmetric key with one of the tools

- Let`s create a symmetric key and use it.

- Import and export, share your keys.

- Build 4 groups and use different tools. Research for encryption tools. The Big 7 Open Source Crypto Study (2016) references a list of all worldwide available encryption tools: Check, if your researched tool is listed there.

- Report to the plenum, how the process has been working out.

- What are the main hints to give to others how to be sucessful with this research and exercise – give criteria for your success.

3 EPOCHS IN CRYPTOGRAPHY DEFINED BY KEY-HANDLING

Since 2019: „Third Epoch" (Bertram/van Dooble 2019)
- Solving the Key Transport Problem: Key Derivation instead of Key Exchange.
- Exponential Encryption (Gasakis/Schmidt 2019).
- Volatile Encryption & Fiasco Forwarding (Fiasco Keys).
- Zero Knowledge Keys for symmetric Encryption: e.g. Secret Streams and Juggerknot Keys.

3. EPOCH IN CRYPTOGRAPHY

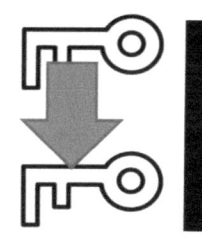 Zero Knowledge with Key Derivation - but Zero Key Transfer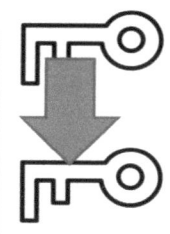

Since 1972: Second Epoch
- Computerbased Public Key Infrastructure (PKI).
- E.g. McEliece PKI & NTRU PKI.
- Asymmetric encryption as new direction.
- Diffie-Hellman Key Exchange (ebda. 1972).
- No exchange of secret keys in PKI (asymmetric Encryption).

2. EPOCH IN CRYPTOGRAPHY

Public Keys

Private Key   Private Key

Historical Encryption: First Epoch
- Shared Secret / One Time Pads / AES-256.
- Symmetric Encryption. Geminis.
- Kerkhoffs' Principle: Keeping the Key secret rather than the Algorithm.

1. EPOCH IN CRYPTOGRAPHY

 Symmetric Keys

ELSE TO KNOW...: RANDOM NUMBERS

- A true random number generator (TRNG) is a device that generates a sequence of numbers or symbols that cannot be reasonably predicted better than by a random chance. Random number generators can be true hardware random-number generators (HRNG), which generate genuinely random numbers, or pseudo-random number generators (PRNG), which generate numbers that look random, but are actually deterministic, and can be reproduced if the state of the PRNG is known.

- Various applications of randomness have led to the development of several different methods for generating random data, of which some have existed since ancient times, among whose ranks are well-known "classic" examples, including the rolling of dice, coin flipping, the shuffling of playing cards.

- Random number generators in software and hardware are often subject to be manipulated to be able to break cryptographic functions.

- The Spot-On Suite contains a function for distributing randomly-generated streams of data. If the Spot-On instance is configured on a system with a TRNG, it may be used for distributing random numbers to weaker devices.

FREQUENCY ANALYSIS: SUBSTITUTION WITHOUT ROTATION?
DISTRIBUTION OF LETTERS IN ENGLISH

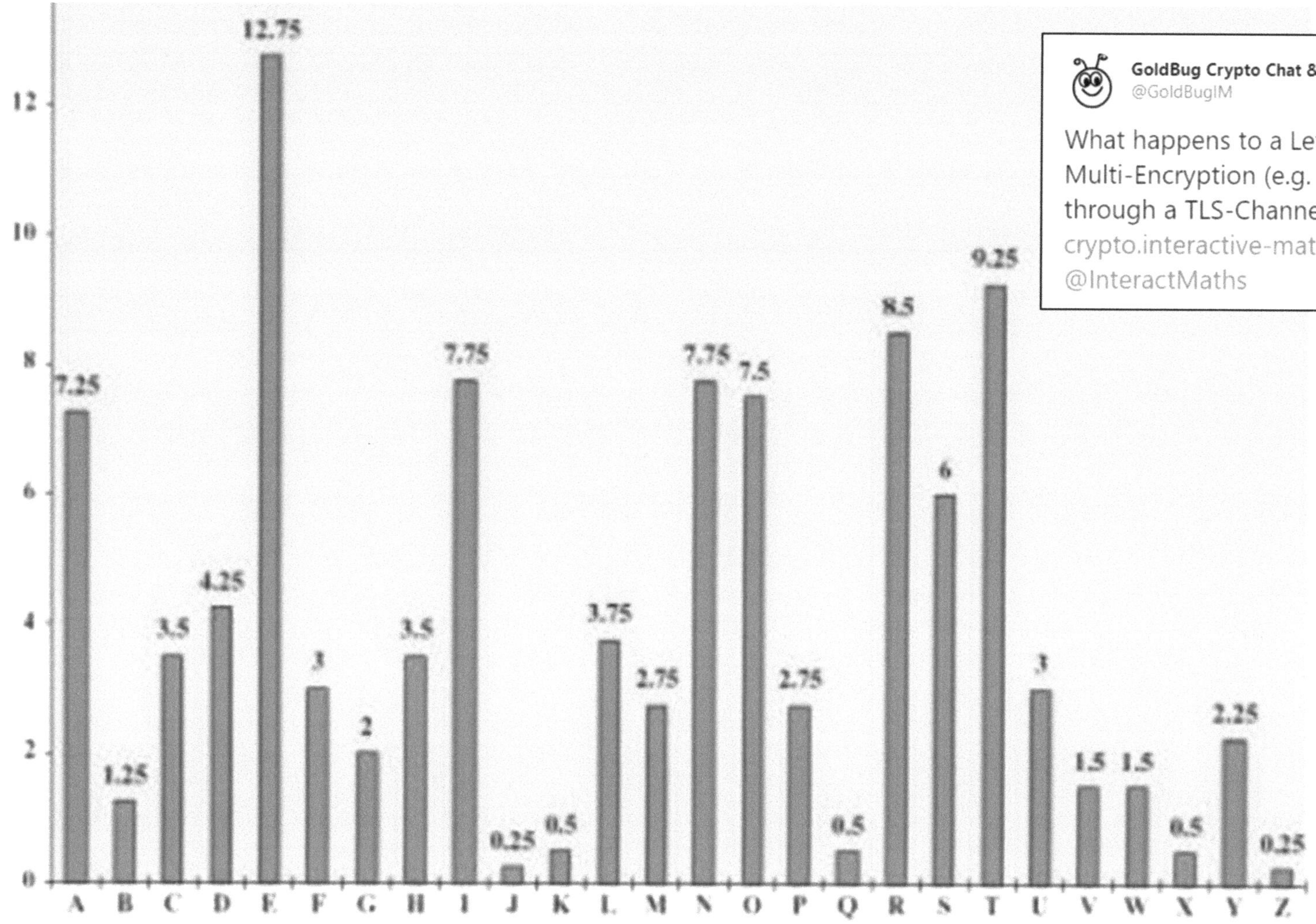

GoldBug Crypto Chat & E-Mail
@GoldBugIM

What happens to a Letter Frequency Analysis within Multi-Encryption (e.g. RSA * NTUR * McEliece) sent through a TLS-Channel?
crypto.interactive-maths.com/frequency-anal...
@InteractMaths

Chart values by letter:
- A: 7.25
- B: 1.25
- C: 3.5
- D: 4.25
- E: 12.75
- F: 3
- G: 2
- H: 3.5
- I: 7.75
- J: 0.25
- K: 0.5
- L: 3.75
- M: 2.75
- N: 7.75
- O: 7.5
- P: 2.75
- Q: 0.5
- R: 8.5
- S: 6
- T: 9.25
- U: 3
- V: 1.5
- W: 1.5
- X: 0.5
- Y: 2.25
- Z: 0.25

https://crypto.interactive-maths.com/frequency-analysis-breaking-the-code.html

Ackermann & Klein: Caesura in Cryptography (2020)

ONE TIME PAD

There is one type of substitution cipher that is absolutely unbreakable.

- The **one-time pad** was invented in 1917 by Joseph Mauborgne and Gilbert Vernam

    - We use a block of shift keys, $(k_1, k_2, \ldots, k_n)$, to encrypt a plaintext, M, of length n, with each shift key being chosen uniformly at random.
    - The encryption is done by adding the key to the message modulo 2, bit by bit. This process is often called exclusive or, XOR.

- Since each shift is random, every ciphertext is equally likely for any plaintext.
- The key has to be as long as the plaintext
- Key distribution & Management is difficult as long not Zero Knowledge methods are used as with Secret Streams or Juggerknot Keys.
- Key should not be re-used.

OTP: Example

- message ='IF'
- then its ASCII code =(1001001 1000110)
- key = (1010110 0110001)
- *Encryption:*
    - 1001001 1000110 plaintext
    - 1010110 0110001 key
    - 0011111 1110110 ciphertext
- *Decryption:*
    - 0011111 1110110 ciphertext
    - 1010110 0110001 key
    - 1001001 1000110 plaintext

ELSE TO KNOW...: HASH FUNCTION

- A hash function is any well-defined procedure or mathematical function that converts a large, possibly variable-sized amount of data into a small datum, usually a single integer that may serve as an index to an array. The values returned by a hash function are called hash values, hash codes, hash sums, checksums or simply hashes.

- A hash function h maps a plaintext x to a fixed-length value x = h(P) called hash value or digest of P

  - Usually x is much smaller in size compared to P.

  - A collision is a pair of plaintexts P and Q that map to the same hash value, h(P) = h(Q)

  - Collisions are unavoidable

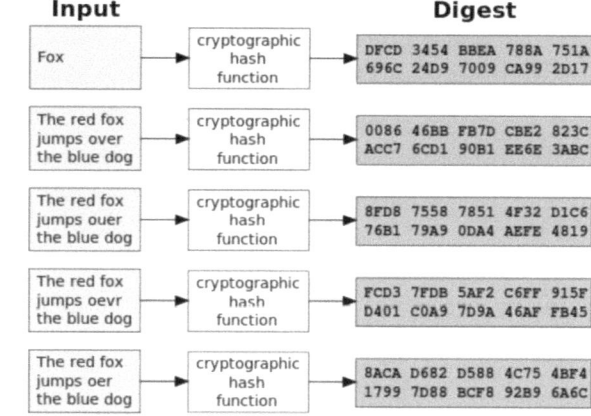

- A cryptographic hash function satisfies additional properties: Collision resistance (aka strong collision resistance)

  - It is hard to find a pair of plaintexts P and Q such that h(Q) = h(P)

Ackermann & Klein: Caesura in Cryptography (2020)

DIGITAL SIGNATURES WITH ENCRYPTION

A digital signature or digital signature scheme is a mathematical scheme for demonstrating the authenticity of a digital message or document. A valid digital signature gives a recipient reason to believe that the message was created by a known sender, and that it was not altered in transit.

1) Alice signs the message with her private key

$$S_A(M)$$

2) Alice encrypts the signed message with Bob's public key and sends it to Bob

$$E_B(S_A(M))$$

3) Bob decrypts the message with his private key

$$D_B(E_B(S_A(M))) = S_A(M)$$

4) Bob verifies with Alice's public key and recovers the message

$$V_A(S_A(M)) = M$$

Ackermann & Klein: Caesura in Cryptography (2020)

MESSAGE AUTHENTICATION CODES (MAC)

- In cryptography, a message authentication code (often MAC) is a short piece of information used to authenticate a message.

- A MAC algorithm, sometimes called a keyed (cryptographic) hash function, accepts as input a secret key and an arbitrary-length message to be authenticated, and outputs a MAC (sometimes known as a *tag*). The MAC value protects both a message's data integrity as well as its authenticity, by allowing verifiers (who also possess the secret key) to detect any changes to the message content.

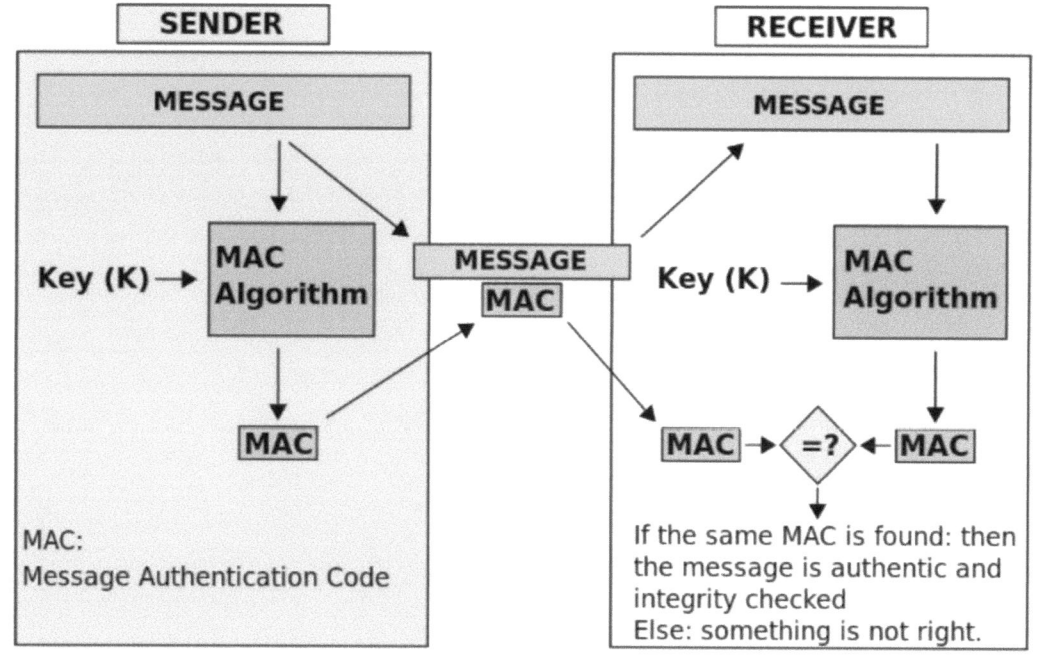

S/MIME & GNUPGP

- Two standards have been established for PKI-based email encryption: S/MIME (Secure / Multipurpose Internet Mail Extensions) and OpenPGP (Pretty Good Privacy).

- Both basically use the same cryptographic methods. However, they differ in the certification of public keys and thus in the trust models. Both standards are not compatible with each other - this means that users of one method cannot exchange signed or encrypted messages with users of the other method.

- S/MIME describes a standard in which so-called X.5096 certificates are used. Public key certification is offered as a service by public trust centers as Certification Authority (CAs).

- Depending on the examination procedure and the associated level of trust, the certificates are chargeable.

- The trust model is hierarchical. The identities are verified via a chain of certificates, from the user certificate to any assigned intermediate CAs to the root CA certificate of the issuing body.

Ackermann & Klein: Caesura in Cryptography (2020)

OPENPGP & GNUPG

- GnuPG is a free software implementation of the OpenPGP standard.

- PGP stands for Pretty Good Privacy.

- PGP is a system for encrypting data, and for creating digital signatures (aka signing).

- Commonly used for e-mail but can be used with any type of data or file or with chat.

- PGP takes a little work to set up. After that, it's easy to use.

- First, focus on the setup part.

RESSOURCES

- GnuPG: http://gnupg.org/
  - Windows / GPG4win: http://gpg4win.org/
  - Linux GnuPG may already be installed. If not, use your package manager (yum, apt-get, zypper, synaptic, aptitude, etc.) to install it.
  - Mac OS https://gpgtools.org/

- Also useful: Thunderbird https://www.mozilla.org/en-US/thunderbird/

- Also useful: Enigmail https://www.enigmail.net/home/index.php

- GPG Tools: http://gpgtools.org/

GNUPG/OPENPGP & WEB OF TRUST

Web of Trust

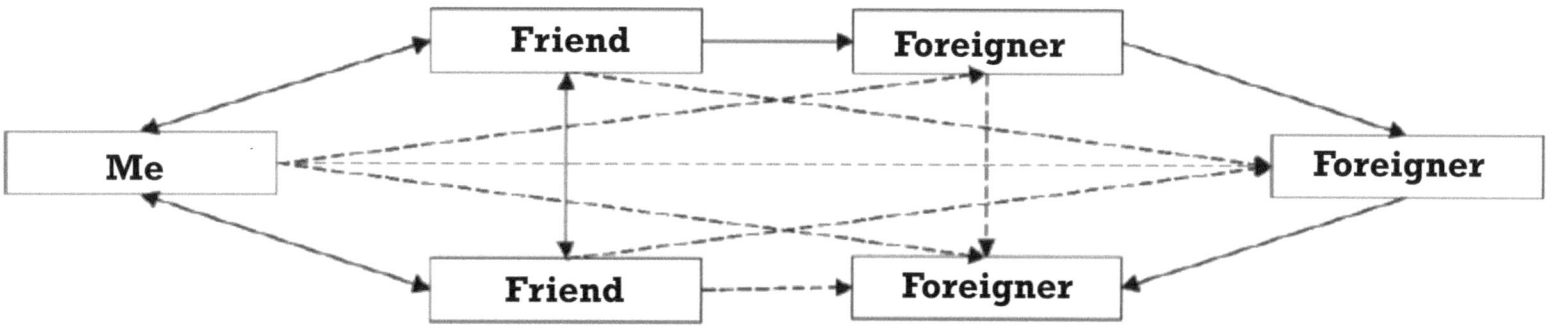

	Schematic representation of the Web of Trust model

- OpenPGP provides that the participants sign their public keys with each other and thereby certify them. This creates a "Web of Trust (WOT)", a network of trust that works without hierarchies.

- GnuPG is the open implementation of the OpenPGP standard defined in RFC 4880. GnuPG allows you to encrypt and sign data and to authenticate. It is written in C and has been initially released in 1999.

- Key pairs are created in-house and public PGP keys are mutually certified by participants, for example at key signing parties.

- PGP users can sign other users' public keys with their own private keys to document their authenticity.

- In contrast to certificates that are only signed by a CA, a PGP key can contain any number of digital signatures.

- Software: e.g. RetroShare.

CRYPTOGRAPHIC CAFETERIA

The Cryptographic Cafeteria - A didactic game for teaching

Consider in your tutorial the idea and feedback that the topic to learners for a presentation should be chosen by naming a number of 1-300 by the learner.

With this page number, a **cryptographic encyclopedia like Nomenclatura** (2019) can thus be used to assign a lecture topic to a quasi-random (and therefore also didactically challenging) topic - namely, using the keyword that follows next on the page mentioned. This educational didactic exercise for the lesson we call "Crypto-Cafeteria" will be designed as a university (and depending on the design also academic) discussion and presentation course and within the 12 sessions of the course the topics randomly from a lexicon curriculum to have chosen, has charm. As in a cafeteria, the page number of an encyclopedia allows the learner to choose a "snack", "eat" content, and report to their peers.

In particular with the rule: A learner may skip a keyword found to the next keyword, if they find a partner in the class who jumps back a keyword and selects the previous keyword. The teacher defines the algorithm of how many keywords should jump forward or backward.

As well as: Two students with consecutive pages, may decide independently to work together only one of the two topics found. Furthermore: If you do not want to give a presentation, you should provide a paper with 10-15 pages afterwards.

This "Balance of Karma in Class" rule should certainly promote team development and joint presentations: particularly content-laden topics should be in a team explored, researched and compared, combined, summarized and conveyed. - After a selection using the Cryptographic Cafeteria method.

A cafeteria model (also cafeteria system or cafeteria principle) is called a form of a model in companies for compensation and benefits. The intention of this model is to increase motivation through individual and free choice within an available portfolio. The system is to be assigned to the cognitive theories of choice in the motivation theories. In the company area, depending on the position, the employee receives a certain amount of points, which they can freely spend on services within the cafeteria system.

In the school area, a defined learning snack can be found as a subject for the lecture, with the help of a freely chosen or random number, in order to first receive a learning offer or a teaching assignment as a multiplier in front of the class.

Source: Bertram / van Dooble (2019:56)

Ackermann & Klein: Caesura in Cryptography (2020)

END-TO-END ENCRYPTION

- End-to-end encryption (E2EE) is a system of communication where only the communicating users can read the messages. In principle, it prevents potential eavesdroppers – including telecom providers, Internet providers, and even the provider of the communication service – from being able to access the cryptographic keys needed to decrypt the conversation.

- In many messaging systems, including email and many chat networks, messages pass through intermediaries and are stored by a third party, from which they are retrieved by the recipient. Even if the messages are encrypted, they are only encrypted 'in transit' to the next point (point-to-point encryption), and are thus accessible by the service provider.

- Keyboards and keyboard App providers might be potential eavesdroppers.

POINT-TO-POINT (TRANSPORT) ENCRYPTION VERSUS END-TO-END ENCRYPTION

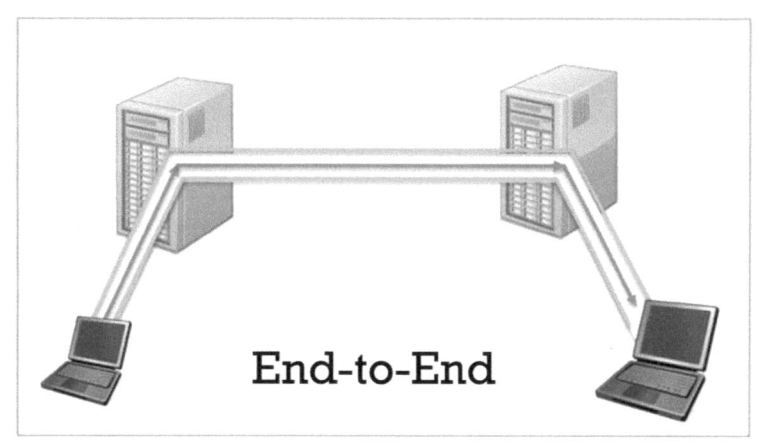

End-to-End

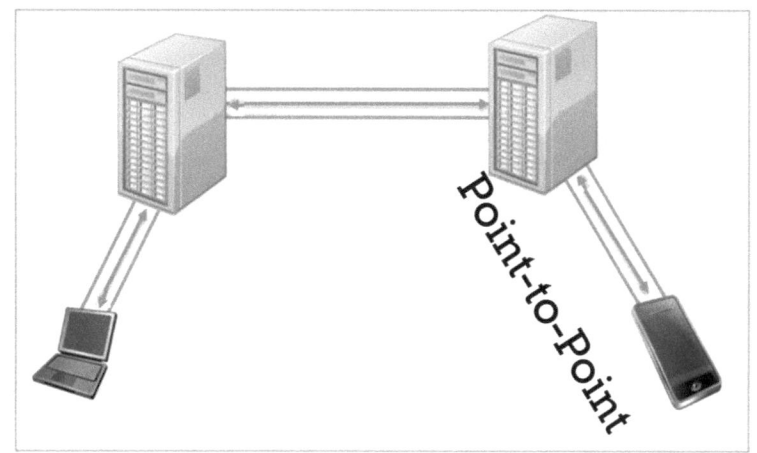

Point-to-Point

- **End-to-end encryption** (E2EE) is a system of communication where only the communicating users can read the messages.

- Even if the messages are encrypted, they are only encrypted 'in transit' to the next point (point-to-point encryption), and are thus accessible by the service provider.

INSTANT PERFECT FORWARD SECRECY (IPFS)

- IPFS is the abbreviation of Instant Perfect Forward Secrecy.

- While Perfect Forward Secrecy, often also called only Forward Secrecy, describes within many applications and as well from a conceptional approach the transmission of ephemeral - this means temporary - keys, it is implicit connected, that this is proceeded one time per online session.

- With the open source Encryption Suite Spot-On and the underlying architecture of the Spot-On Kernel a new paradigm has been implemented: Forward Secrecy or Perfect Forward Secrecy, has developed further to Instant Perfect Forward Secrecy (IPFS).

- While Forward Secrecy means to be able to neglect to have used a certain key in the past if one further key is compromised, this concept addresses to end-to-end encryption.

- With Instant Perfect Forward Secrecy the Cryptographic Calling comes into the frame: A user is able to renew the end-to-end encrypting credentials like in a phone call: Instantly and several times within a session the user should be able to renew temporary keys for end-to-end encryption. An even further development of this concept has been taken place by the development of Fiasco, a mechanism which stores a full bundle of keys within one session to be used for future deciphering. (Fiasco is hence more advanced than the Double Ratchet Algo).

- The end-to-end-encryption with temporary keys can be changed at any time, this means also per any second. This describes the term of Instant Perfect Forward Secrecy (IPFS).

- Via a so-called "Call" the end-to-end-encryption can be renewed: Instantly. Also, the term of a "call" for the transmission of a to-be-created or to-be-renewed end-to-end-encryption has been introduced by the application Spot-On into Cryptography.

CRYPTOGRAPHIC CALLING

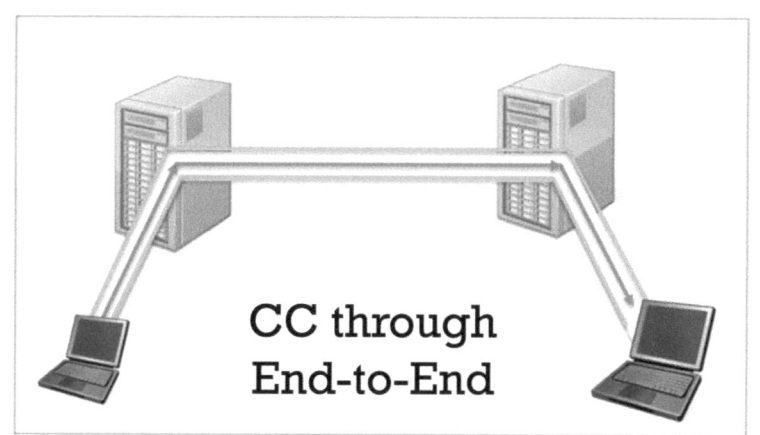

CC through
End-to-End

- The Cryptographic Calling describes the process to create an End-to-End encryption.

- It should be for the user as easy as to call a friend with a phone.

- Instantly, as well within the session, two users can request new credentials for the encryption.

- The Cryptographic Calling provides several methods to create the encryption.

- E.g. through a secure channel A a new key is sent and agreed. The new key created a new secure channel B. The key for next new secure channel C can be sent over channel A or B.

- New keys can be symmetric or asymmetric.

- E.g. the Two-Way-Calling creates a symmetric passphrase, to which each communication partner brings in 50 % of the passphrase.

- The agreement protocol of Cryptographic Calling creates an instant definition of a new key on both sides.

CRYPTOGRAPHIC CALLING:
METHODS

Ackermann & Klein: Caesura in Cryptography (2020)

Figure 45: Overview of the different types of Cryptographic Calling with respective criteria

Criteria	Asymmet-ric Calling	Forward Secrecy Calling	Symmetric Calling	SMP Calling	Secret Streams	Fiasco Forwarding	2-Way Calling
TLS/SSL-Connection	YES	YES	YES	YES	YES	YES	YES
Permanent asymmet-ric Chat/E-Mail Key	YES	YES	YES	YES	YES	YES	YES
Symmetric AES as Gemini	NO	NO	YES	NO	NO	NO	NO
Half AES + Half AES	NO	NO	NO	NO	NO	NO	YES
Secret SMP Password	NO	NO	NO	YES	YES	NO	NO
Ephemeral/temp. Chat/E-Mail PKI-Key	NO	YES	NO	NO	NO	NO	NO
Forward Secrecy as Pre-Condition	NO	YES	YES	NO	NO	YES	NO
Instant Perfect Forward Secrecy as result	YES	YES	YES	YES	YES	YES	YES
Several keys as a result	NO	NO	NO	NO	YES	YES	NO

Source: Edwards 2019

CRYPTOGRAPHIC CALLING:
2-WAY-CALLING

Figure 09: Two-Way Calling

> ## Two-Way Calling
>
> Spot-On and further Clients like GoldBug utilizing the Echo kernel implement a plain two-pass key-distribution system. The protocol is defined as follows:
>
> 1.   A peer generates 128-bit AES and 256-bit SHA-512 keys via the system's cryptographic random number generator.
> 2.   Using the destination's public key, the peer encapsulates the two keys via the hybrid cryptographic system, as it has been described above for the Echo Protocol.
> 3.   The destination peer receives the data, records it, and generates separate keys as in step 1.
> 4.   The destination peer transmits the encapsulated keys to the originating peer as in step 2.
>
> Once the protocol is executed, the two peers shall possess identical authentication and encryption keys. Please note that duplicate half-keys are allowed. The passphrase, which will be then used for the end-to-end encryption, is generated by 50% of the one peer and 50% of the other peer.

Source: Spot-On Documentation 2014.

Source: Edwards 2019

Key in English: Thats my Kung Fu
(16 ASCII characters, 1 byte each)

Translation into Hex:

T	h	a	t	s		m	y		K	u	n	g		F	u
54	68	61	74	73	20	6D	79	20	4B	75	6E	67	20	46	75

Key in Hex (128 bits):
54 68 61 74 73 20 6D 79 20 4B 75 6E 67 20 46 75

ALICE PART 2

Plaintext in English: Two One Nine Two
(16 ASCII characters, 1 byte each)

T	w	o		O	n	e		N	i	n	e		T	w	o
54	77	6F	20	4F	6E	65	20	4E	69	6E	65	20	54	77	6F

Plaintext in Hex (128 bits):
54 77 6F 20 4F 6E 65 20 4E 69 6E 65 20 54 77 6F

BOB PART 1

54 77 6F 20 4F 6E 65 20   +   20 4B 75 6E 67 20 46 75

Commonly defined symmetric key on both sides:

54 77 6F 20 4F 6E 65 20 20 4B 75 6E 67 20 46 75

MULTI-ENCRYPTED LONG DISTANCE CALLING (MELODICA)

- With the MELODICA feature in GoldBug Secure Messenger the user calls the friend cryptographically and sends a new end-to-end encrypting Gemini (AES-256-Key).

- The Key is sent over your asymmetric encryption of the Master key. This is a secure way, as all other plaintext transfers like: email, spoken over phone or in other messengers, have to be regarded as unsafe and recorded.

- MELODICA stands for: Multi Encrypted Long Distance Calling.

- The idea is to call a friend even over a long distance of the Echo protocol and exchange over secure asymmetric encryption a Gemini (AES-256 key) to establish an end-to-end encrypted channel.

- The MELODICA button was a graphical symbol for the beginning of the implementations for and development of Cryptographic Calling.

Figure 37: The MELODICA Button since 2013

MELODICA Button

MELODICA stands for "Multi-Encrypted LOng DIstance CAll-ing" – that means: "Multiple-Encrypted Calls over a Long Distance". The MELODICA symbol is therefore a piano keyboard as musical instrument and was first implemented in GoldBug's User Interface of Spot-On.

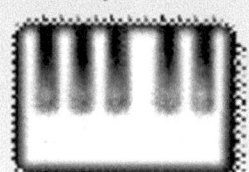

Source: Edwards 2019

THRICE-BLESSED SUPERENCIPHERMENT: HYBRID & MULTI-ENCRYPTION

Multi-Encryption is the process of encrypting an already encrypted message one or more times, either using the same or a different algorithm (Nomenclatura 2019: 249).

- With the exception of the one-time pad, no cipher has been theoretically proven to be unbreakable.

- Assumption that **more than once converted text** is more secure than a just one time encrypted text (Edwards 2019:33).

- Is thrice-RSA (RSA * RSA * RSA) converted text less secure than thrice-blessed and encrypted text (RSA * McEliece * NTRU)? And is the order important for security: (RSA * McEliece * NTRU) versus (McEliece * RSA * NTRU)?

- Some authors assume multi-encryption is not needed – whithout giving prooving examples – which leads to the assumption that multi-encryption is a big **complexity for cryptoanalysts** (Ritter 1995).

Triqueta

MULTI-ENCRYPTION
A TO BE DEEPEND RESEARCH FIELD

- Examples of Multiple Encryption are found e.g. in the applications **Spot-On Encryption Suite**, GoldBug Messenger and within Fiasco Keys of the Fiasco-Forwarding function of the Smoke Crypto Chat Messenger (Spot-On 2011, Edwards 2018, Smoke 2017).

- **Hybrid Encryption** often refers to an asymmetric encryption of an already symmetric encrypted message (or vice versa) – though it could refer also to a message, converted by RSA and then by McEliece (Bertram 2018:19).

- Multi-Encryption is **a to deepend research field** in regard of the since 2016 as broken considered RSA algorithm (NIST 2016).

- Historically "**Floradora**" (Filby 1995) was a doubly enciphered diplomatic code used during the Second World War and one of the first Multi-Encryptions.

Ackermann & Klein: Caesura in Cryptography (2020)

Your assumptions, opinions & research on **Multi-Encryption?**

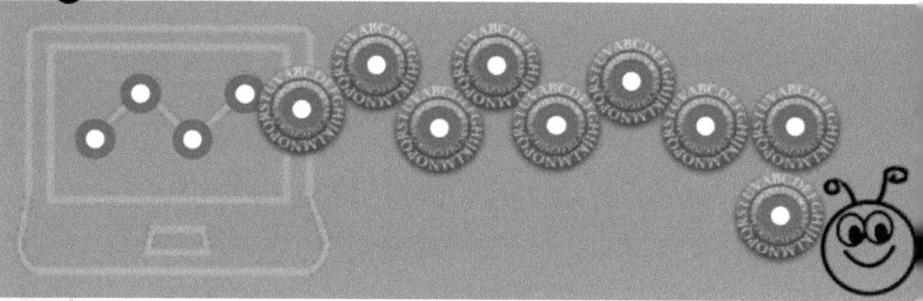

Exercise:
Let's test one of the tools for Multi-Encryption
Adding an AES-based passphrase
to an already PKI-encrypted e-mail.

REPLEO

- With a REPLEO the own public key is encrypted with the already received public key of a friend, so that the own public key can be transferred to the friend in a protected way.

- The REPLEO is the basis for AutoCrypt as an automatic key exchange.

- AutoCrypt refers to the protocol definitions of a REPLEO and the EPKS protocol originally invented by the Spot-on Project.

- A REPLEO hides the own public key from public by using an encryption method.

- The EPKS Protocol is the Echo Public Key Sharing Protocol, which allows to send the own key over an existing encrypted connection to one or several friends.

- These protocols have been overtaken by other projects in an automated way for an e-mail reply with public keys.

- That means two users of the same e-mail client exchange the public encryption key and are from that point of time secured for all further communication. The EPKS Protocol provided this many years before the Term AutoCrypt went public.

- Other project also copied this invention under the Name KeySync.

- The new process is, that the key is not stored and searched on a Key server, but sent from node to node in a secure channel, either by manual sent-out or an automated exchange of two nodes, e.g. e-mail-clients or Spot-On Clients over the EPKS protocol.

- EPKS automatically integrates within an EPKS-Community the shared public keys.

EPKS-CHANNELS:
ECHO PUBLIC KEY SHARE PROTOCOL

- Echo Public Key Share (EPKS) is a function implemented in Spot-On Encryption Suite to share public encryption keys over the Echo Network. It is an elegant compliment to the Echo introduced by Mr. Schmidt.

- This allows a group to share keys over secure channels so that a classical key server it not needed. It is a way of key exchange to a group or one individual user.

- The key exchange (also known as "key establishment") is any method in cryptography by which cryptographic keys are exchanged between users, allowing use of a cryptographic algorithm. If sender and receiver wish to exchange encrypted messages, each must be equipped to encrypt messages to be sent and decrypt messages received.

- The nature of the equipping: their require depends on the encryption technique they might use. If they use a code, both will require a copy of the same codebook. If they use a cipher, they will need appropriate keys. If the cipher is a symmetric key cipher, both will need a copy of the same key.

- In an asymmetric key cipher with the public/private key property, both will need the other's public key. The key exchange problem is how to exchange whatever keys or other information are needed so that no one else can obtain a copy. Historically, this required trusted couriers, diplomatic bags, or some other secure channel. With the advent of public key / private key cipher algorithms, the encrypting key (aka public key) could be made public, since (at least for high quality algorithms) no one without the decrypting key (aka, the private key) could decrypt the message.

- Diffie-Hellman key exchange: In 1976, Whitfield Diffie and Martin Hellman published a cryptographic protocol, (Diffie-Hellman key exchange), which allows users to establish 'secure channels' on which to exchange keys, even if an Opponent is monitoring that communication channel.

- However, D-H key exchange did not address the problem of being sure of the actual identity of the person (or 'entity'). EPKS channels enable to exchange (symmetric and asymmetric) keys within a network as a broadcast without server storage.

- EPKS channels - and also BUZZ rooms - work on the same principle of symmetric encryption: The channel can be known to a community group or just one (other) individual person.

FROM REPLEO & EPKS TO AUTOCRYPT

- AutoCrypt is an automatic key exchange.

- This has originally been invented by the Spot-on Project and refers to the protocol definitions of a REPLEO and the EPKS protocol. A REPLEO is the method to encrypt the own public key with the received public key of a friend. That hides the own public key from public by using an encryption method.

- The EPKS Protocol is the Echo Public Key Sharing Protocol, which allows to send the own key over an existing encrypted connection to one or several friends.

- The EPKS protocol has been invented in the Spot-On project and GoldBug Project and has been overtaken by other projects in an automated way for an e-mail reply with public keys. That means two users of the same e-mail client exchange the public encryption key and are from that point of time secured for all further communication.

- The EPKS Protocol provided this many years before the Term AutoCrypt went public. Other project also copied this invention under the Name KeySync.

- The new process is, that the key is not stored and searched on a Key server, but sent from node to node in a secure channel, either by manual sent-out or an automated exchange of two nodes, e.g. e-mail-clients or Spot-On Clients over the EPKS protocol.

- EPKS automatically integrates within an EPKS-Community the shared public keys.

Ackermann & Klein: Caesura in Cryptography (2020)

BEYOND CRYPTOGRAPHIC ROUTING THE ECHO PROTOCOL

- Spot-On introduced the Echo - or: Echo-Protocol. The Echo is a malleable concept.

- That is, an implementation does not require rigid details. Each model may adhere to their own peculiar obligations.

- The Echo functions on the elementary persuasion that information is dispersed over multiple or singular passages and channel endpoints evaluate the suitability of the received data. Because data may become intolerable, Spot-On implements its own congestion control algorithm. Received messages that meet some basic criteria are labeled and duplicates are discarded. Advanced models may define more sophisticated congestion-avoidance algorithms based upon their interpretations of the Echo.

- The Echo combines encryption and graph theory: With the Echo Protocol is meant - simply put — that first, every message transmission is encrypted and second, in the Echo Network, each connection node sends each message to each connected neighbor. As third criterion for the Echo Protocol can be added, that there is a special feature when unpacking the encrypted capsule: The capsules have neither a receiver nor sender information included - and here they are different from TCP packets.

- The message is identified by the hash of the original message (compared to the conversion text of all known keys in the node) as to whether the message should be displayed and readable to the recipient in the user interface or not. For this so-called "Echo Match" see even more detailed at referring keyword. Spot-On Encryption Suite provides two modes of operation for the general Echo: Full Echo and Half Echo. The Full Echo permits absolute data flow. The Half Echo defines an agreement between two endpoints.

- Within this agreement, information from other endpoints is prohibited from traveling along the private channel.

- The Echo protocol means from an operational view: you send only encrypted messages, but you send your to-be-send-message to all of your connected friends. They do the same.

- You maintain your own network, everyone has every message and you try to decrypt every message. In case you can read and unwrap it, it is a message for you. Otherwise you share the message with all your friends and the message remains encrypted. Echo is very simple, and the principle is many years old — nothing new: As Echo uses HTTP/S as a protocol, there is no forwarding or routing of messages: no IPs are forwarded, e.g. like it is if the user sends the own message e.g. from the home laptop to the own webserver.

- The process starts at each destination new — as the user defines it. The Echo protocol provided by the application Spot-On has nothing to do with RFC 862. A new Echo protocol RFC has to be written or re-newed and extended
  — with or without that RFC-Number it refers to a (P2P or F2F) network.

Ackermann & Klein: Caesura in Cryptography (2020)

WITHIN THE ECHO: ENCRYPTION MEETS GRAPH-THEORY

Encryption Layers:

- 1: Symmetric Encryption (PKI).

- 2: Asymmetric Encryption (e.g. AES/OTP).

- 3: Sent through HTTPS.

Echo Protocol: Beyond Cryptographic Routing

- Every nodes sends to every neighbour.

- Echo Match: Compare hash of original message with converted message hash of any given key.

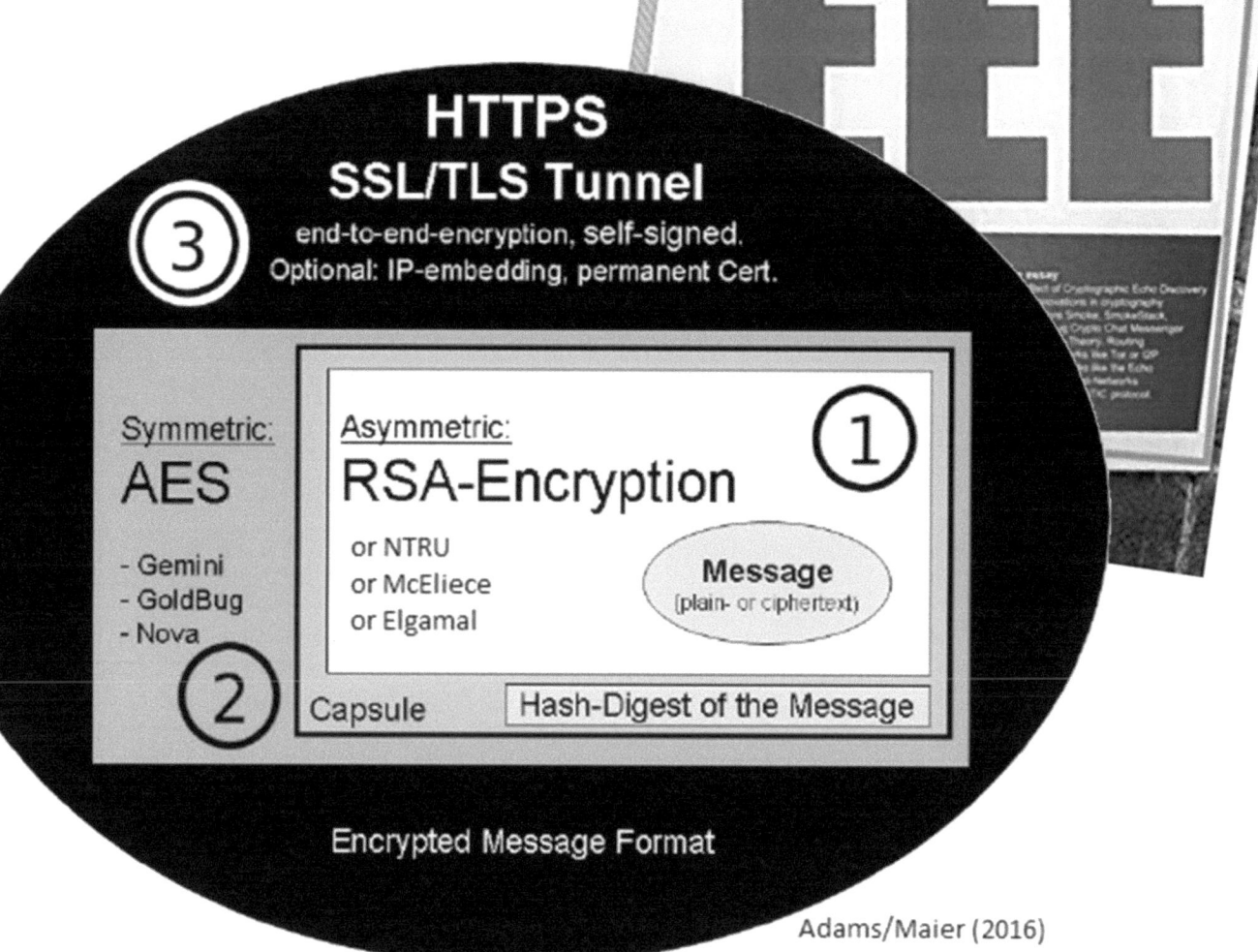

Adams/Maier (2016)

Literature: Adams/Maier 2016, Edwards 2019, Gasakis/Schmidt 2018

Ackermann & Klein: Caesura in Cryptography (2020)

ECHO ENCAPSULATION / ECHO CAPSULE: DESCRIPTION OF THE GRAPHIC & PROCESS

- *(1) First level of encryption: The message is encrypted, and the cipher text of the message is hashed and then the asymmetric key (e.g. with the McEliece or RSA algorithm) can also be used to encrypt the symmetric keys. In an intermediate step, the encrypted text and the hash digest of the message are bundled into a capsule and packed together. It follows the paradigm: Encrypt-then-MAC. To prove to the recipient that the ciphertext has not been corrupted, the hash digest is first formed before the ciphertext is decrypted.*

- *(3) Third level of encryption: Then this capsule can be transmitted via a secure SSL/TLS connection to the communication partner.*

- *(2) Second level of encryption: Optionally, there is also the option of symmetrically encrypting the first-level capsule with an AES-256, which is comparable to a shared, 32-character password. Hybrid encryption is then added to multiple encryptions.*

THE ECHO MATCH

Ackermann & Klein: Caesura in Cryptography (2020)

The Echo Match is a specific cryptographic process to check the provided hash of the original message with the hash of the conversion of the ciphertext with a specific key.

If both hashes are the same, the right key has been chosen. Because the hash function cannot be inverted, the provided hash of the original plaintext message does not provide any information about this message.

Only if both hashes are the same, the conversion from cipher text to plaintext has been successful and the right user with the right key can read the message.

This requires that each given key must be tried out and if the message cannot be converted successfully, that the message has to be provided to all known network connections and nodes to be tried out there: the message cannot be read by this node with given keys.

Practical Example and Process Description

of the Echo-Match

Sender A hashed his original text to a hash 123456789, encrypts the text and packs the crypto-text and hash of the original message into the capsule (before he adds an AES-Password and sends it out via a TLS/SSL connection). Recipient 1 converts the received encoded text of the capsule to a (supposed) plaintext, but this has the hash 987654321 and is therefore not identical to the supplied original text hash of 123456789. This is repeated with all available keys of all friends of the recipient 1. Since all hash comparisons, however, were unsuccessful, he re-packs the message again and sends it on. The message is obviously not for him or from one of his friends. Recipient 2 now also converts the received, encrypted text to a (supposed) plaintext, this has the hash 123456789 and is thus identical to the supplied original text hash of 123456789, the decoding was apparently successful with one of the existing keys of his friends and therefore the message is displayed on the screen of this receiver.

Figure 25: Example for the Echo-Match
(within a simplified process description).

IT'S A MATCH

EXPONENTIAL ENCRYPTION
AMALGAMATION OF GRAPH-THEORY & MULTI-ENCRYPTION

Exponential Encryption

- Exponential Encryption is a term coined by the analysts and authors Meke Gasakis and Max Schmidt in their book about „The New Era of Exponential Encryption" (EEE), in which they analyze based on the Echo Protocol the trends and their vision to provide exponential options for encryption and decryption processes in combination with graph-theory within Echo networks. Here each node sends each message to each known neighbor, which multiplicities the options like a rice corn – according to a popular story – doubling at each field of a chess board.

- Exponential Encryption brings network theory including graph theory and encryption together and multiplies the options.

- Also, a description of working together in community driven projects is described and the foundation of Cryptographic Discovery, the learning of machines/nodes by Cryptographic Tokens, has been founded within that book. Four arms of development are identified by the authors based on their analysis:

- *Metadata-Resistance:* Avoidance of meta-data recording e.g. by usage of protocols minimizing this.

- *Multi-Encryption:* Hybrid and/or Multi-Encryption means: Ciphertext is converted to ciphertext once more or several Algorithms are deployed.

- *Diversity of Crypto-DNA:* Manual definition of parameters for individual encryption-options are enable for the user, e.g. by means of Cryptographic Calling or Instant Perfect Forward Secrecy (IPFS) or End-to-End encryption in general.

- *Quantum-Resistance: e.g. with NTRU and McEliece algorithms* - Change of the algorithms for more security in spite of quantum computing.

4 ARMS IN THE ERA OF EXPONENTIAL ENCRYPTION

- Metadata Resistance

- Multi-Encryption

- Diversity of Crypto-DNA

- Quantum-Resistance: with NTRU & McEliece

Ackermann & Klein: Caesura in Cryptography (2020)

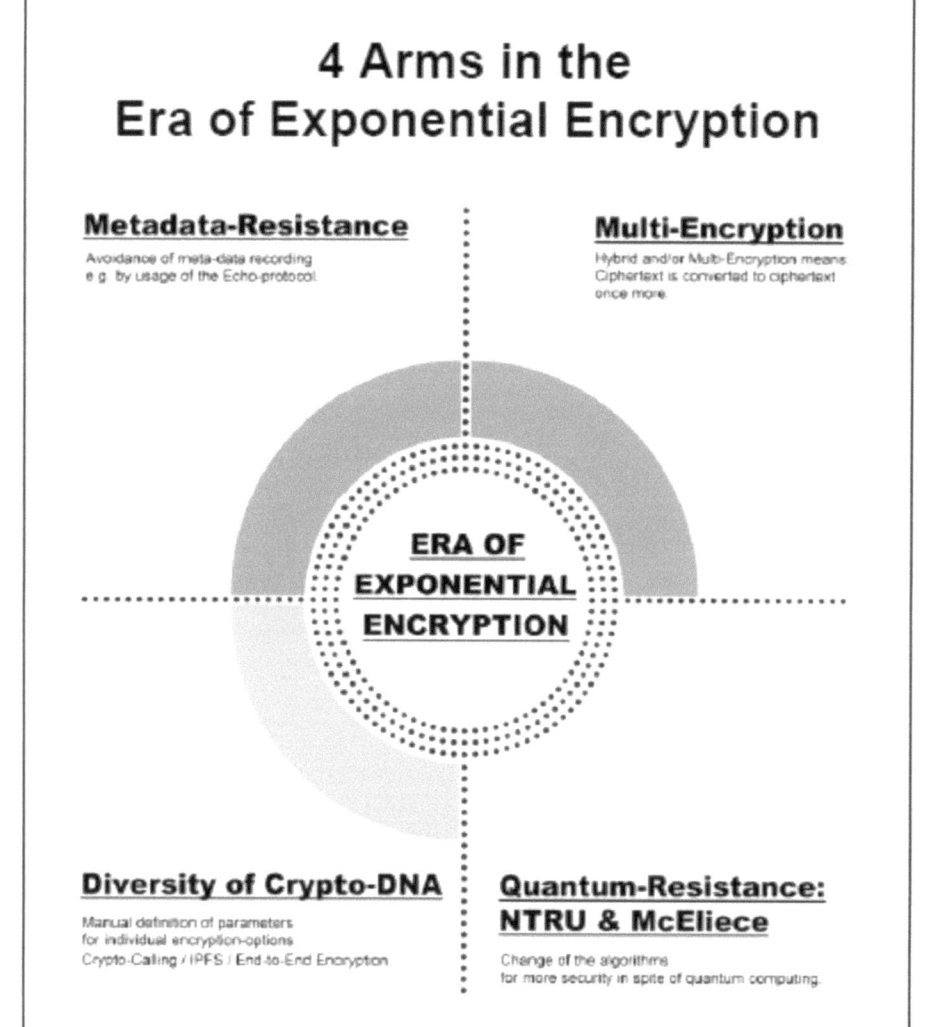

Source: Gasakis / Schmidt 2018

CRYPTOGRAPHYIC DISCOVERY (CD)

- Cryptographic Discovery describes the method of an Echo-ing Protocol to find nodes in an Echo Network. Peers are aware of other peers and their cryptographic identities based on a cryptographic discovery within the network.

- Nodes inform other nodes about their neighbors, so that they can be addressed.

- Cryptographic discovery is then a mechanism which allows servers to lighten the computational and data responsibilities of e.g. mobile devices. It is implemented in the Messenger Smoke and its server software SmokeStack.

- Shortly after a Smoke instance connects to a SmokeStack service, the Smoke instance shares some nonprivate material. The material allows a SmokeStack server to transfer messages to their correct destinations.

- To mitigate replay attacks, Smoke offers SmokeStack instances random identity streams during message-retrieval requests. The identity streams self-expire. Nodes are sprinkled with routing information.

- *Gasakis / Schmidt (2018).*

Ackermann & Klein: Caesura in Cryptography (2020)

CRYPTOGRAPHYIC DISCOVERY
& THE SECRED SPRINKLING EFFECT

Ackermann & Klein: Caesura in Cryptography (2020)

Figure 04:   SECRED - Sprinkling Effect (SE)
& Cryptographic Echo Discovery (CRED)
via the Echo Protocol

The sprinkling effect (SE) can be understood as a watering that can feed and nourish a flower. The collected information is passed on by a node to the neighbors. Each neighbor participating in the Cryptographic Echo Discovery distributes this complementary CRED information to the other neighbors. So, every neighbor is sprinkled. S E C R E D is an acronym for the term: Sprinkling Effect via CRyptographic Echo Discovery.

Description of the sprinkling effect based on the Spot-On Project Documentation (07/2016)

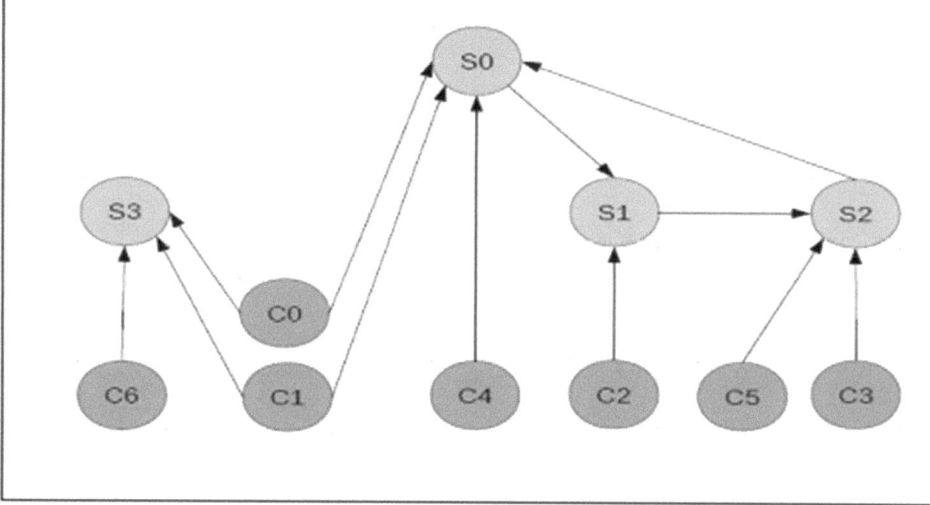

Source: Gasakis /Schmidt (2018:49)

VOLATILE ENCRYPTION
FIASCO FORWARDING: FIASCO KEYS

- Volatile Encryption

See also Fiasco Forwarding. The extremely volatile design using Fiasco keys or Fiasco Forwarding has significant advantages over other, more schematic protocol implementations.

Volatile does not mean that the encryption is shaky or uncertain, but volatile encryption refers to changing and temporary keys that are volatile, fleeting and evaporating - thus not only decreasing the possibilities of decryption, but also multiplying the necessary decryption attempts per message and any decryption opportunities are reduced.

This approach can also be found in the Steam (was: Vapor) Protocol design. See also Steam / Vapor Protocol within the Smoke Chat Client.

SOCIALIST MILLIONAIRE PROTOCOL / SMP

- A form of authentication by entering a password on both sides
- without transferring this secret („*Honolulu*") over the Internet.

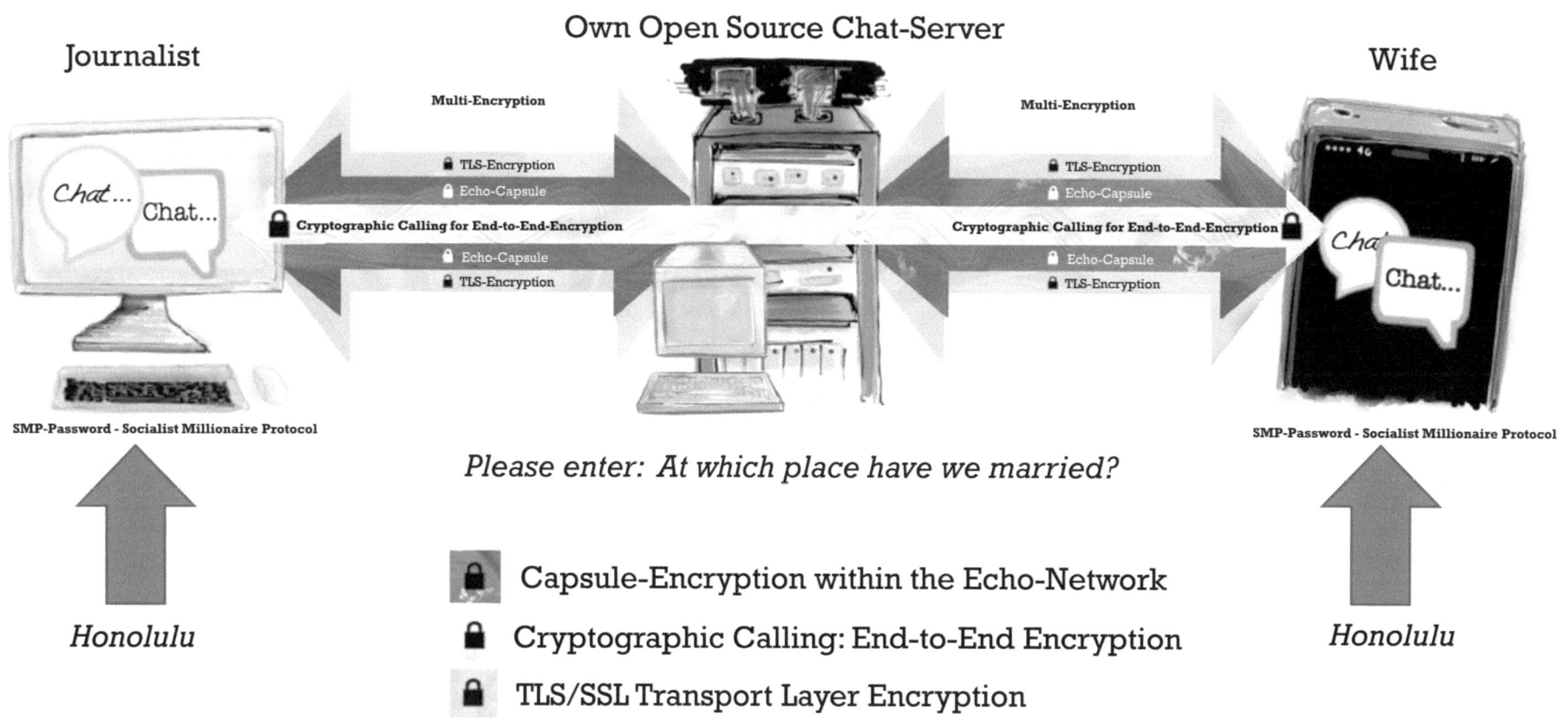

Own Open Source Chat-Server

Journalist

Wife

Multi-Encryption

Multi-Encryption

🔒 TLS-Encryption

🔒 Echo-Capsule

🔒 Cryptographic Calling for End-to-End-Encryption

🔒 Echo-Capsule

🔒 TLS-Encryption

🔒 TLS-Encryption

🔒 Echo-Capsule

🔒 Cryptographic Calling for End-to-End-Encryption

🔒 Echo-Capsule

🔒 TLS-Encryption

Chat... Chat...

Chat... Chat...

SMP-Password - Socialist Millionaire Protocol

SMP-Password - Socialist Millionaire Protocol

Honolulu

Honolulu

Please enter: At which place have we married?

🔒 Capsule-Encryption within the Echo-Network

🔒 Cryptographic Calling: End-to-End Encryption

🔒 TLS/SSL Transport Layer Encryption

SOCIALIST MILLIONAIRE PROTOCOL

STATE MACHINE GRAPHICAL OVERVIEW

ALSO USED FOR KEY DERIVATION

Ackermann & Klein: Caesura in Cryptography (2020)

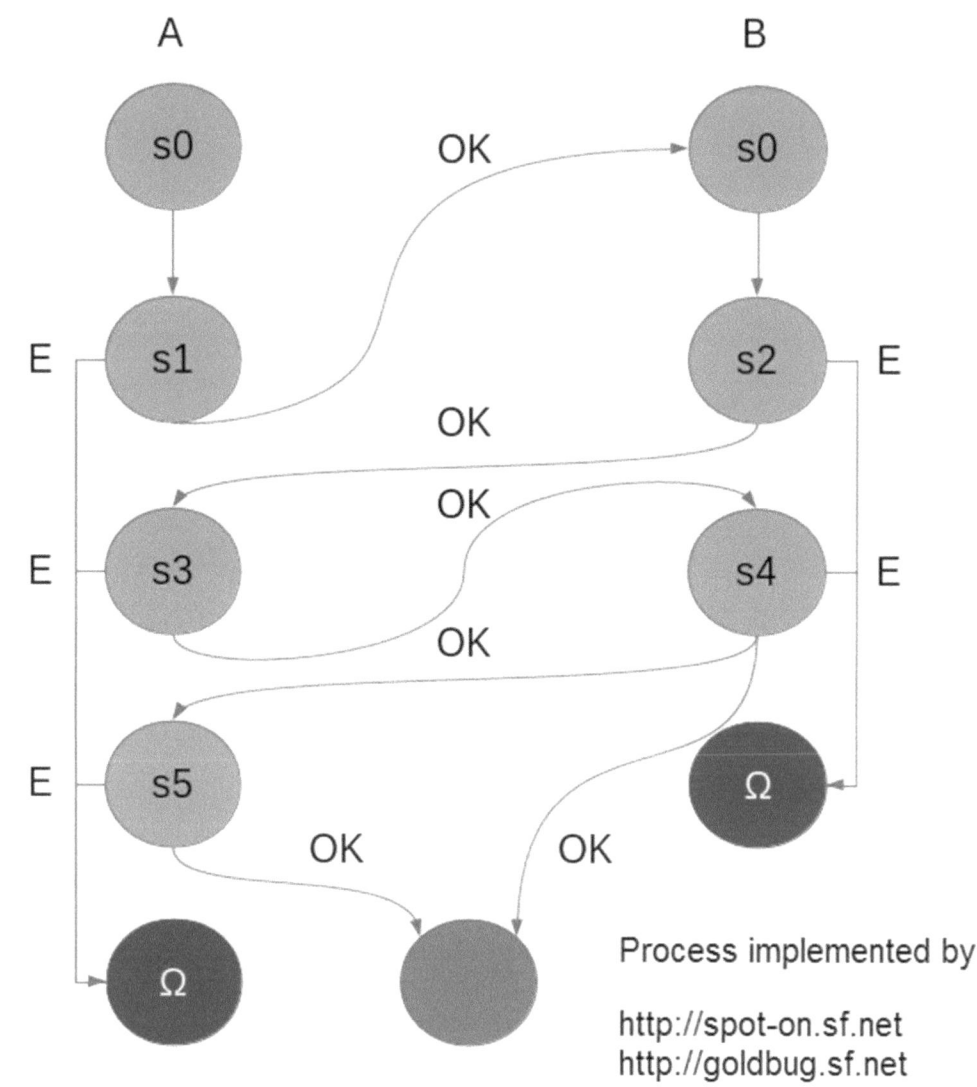

SMP - Socialist Millionaire Protocol
State Machine

Process implemented by

http://spot-on.sf.net
http://goldbug.sf.net

SOCIALIST MILLIONAIRE PROTOCOL / SMP

- Spot-On Encryption Suite includes an asynchronous implementation of the Socialist Millionaire Protocol Spot-On uses the SHA-512 of the secrets as the x and y components. SHA-512 is also used during proof assembly and validation.

- Assuming that Alice begins the exchange:

- Alice:
  1. Picks random exponents a_2 and a_3
  2. Sends Bob $g_{2a} = g_1{}^{a_2}$ and $g_{3a} = g_1{}^{a_3}$
- Bob:
  1. Picks random exponents b_2 and b_3
  2. Computes $g_{2b} = g_1{}^{b_2}$ and $g_{3b} = g_1{}^{b_3}$
  3. Computes $g_2 = g_{2a}{}^{b_2}$ and $g_3 = g_{3a}{}^{b_3}$
  4. Picks random exponent r
  5. Computes $P_b = g_3{}^{r}$ and $Q_b = g_1{}^{r} g_2{}^{y}$
  6. Sends Alice g_{2b}, g_{3b}, P_b and Q_b

- Alice:
  1. Computes $g_2 = g_{2b}{}^{a_2}$ and $g_3 = g_{3b}{}^{a_3}$
  2. Picks random exponent s
  3. Computes $P_a = g_3{}^{s}$ and $Q_a = g_1{}^{s} g_2{}^{x}$
  4. Computes $R_a = (Q_a / Q_b)^{a_3}$
  5. Sends Bob P_a, Q_a and R_a

- Bob:
  1. Computes $R_b = (Q_a / Q_b)^{b_3}$
  2. Computes $R_{ab} = R_a{}^{b_3}$
  3. Checks whether $R_{ab} == (P_a / P_b)$
  4. Sends Alice R_b
- Alice:
  1. Computes $R_{ab} = R_b{}^{a_3}$
  2. Checks whether $R_{ab} == (P_a / P_b)$

- If everything is done correctly, then R_{ab} should hold the value of (P_a / P_b) times $(g_2{}^{a_3 b_3})^{(x - y)}$, which means that the test at the end of the protocol will only succeed if x == y. Further, since $g_2{}^{a_3 b_3}$ is a random number not known to any party, if x is not equal to y, no other information is revealed. See also a detailed description under https://otr.cypherpunks.ca/Protocol-v3-4.0.0.html.

Ackermann & Klein: Caesura in Cryptography (2020)

7 Steps of **Key-Complexity** in Cryptography:
Historical Development of Next Generation Best Practices

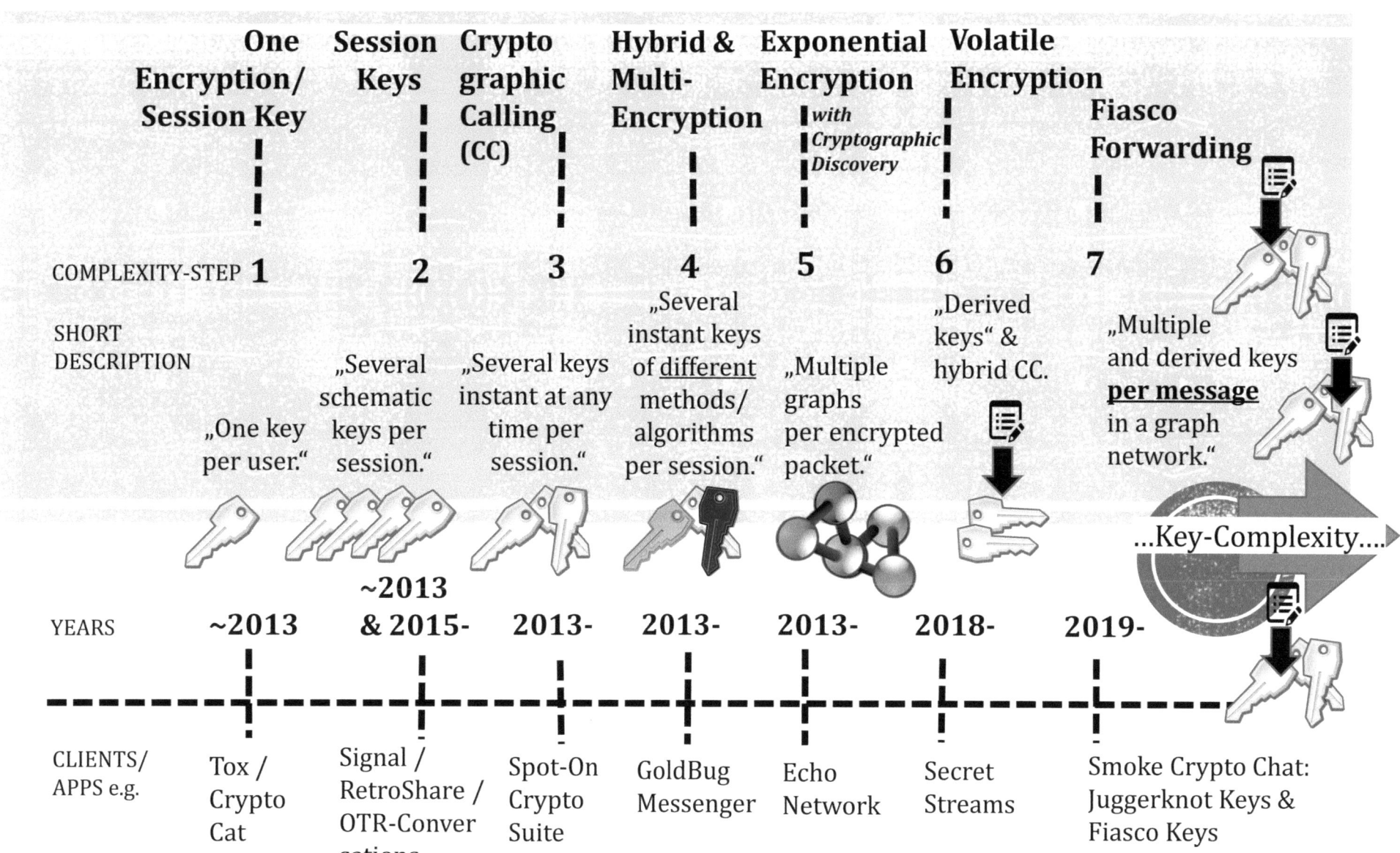

	One Encryption/ Session Key	Session Keys	Crypto graphic Calling (CC)	Hybrid & Multi- Encryption	Exponential Encryption *with Cryptographic Discovery*	Volatile Encryption	Fiasco Forwarding
COMPLEXITY-STEP	1	2	3	4	5	6	7
SHORT DESCRIPTION	„One key per user."	„Several schematic keys per session."	„Several keys instant at any time per session."	„Several instant keys of different methods/ algorithms per session."	„Multiple graphs per encrypted packet."	„Derived keys" & hybrid CC.	„Multiple and derived keys per message in a graph network."
YEARS	~2013	~2013 & 2015-	2013-	2013-	2013-	2018-	2019-
CLIENTS/ APPS e.g.	Tox / Crypto Cat	Signal / RetroShare / OTR-Conver sations	Spot-On Crypto Suite	GoldBug Messenger	Echo Network	Secret Streams	Smoke Crypto Chat: Juggerknot Keys & Fiasco Keys

...Key-Complexity....

END OF LIFE-CYCLE: RSA-ENCRYPTION ✝

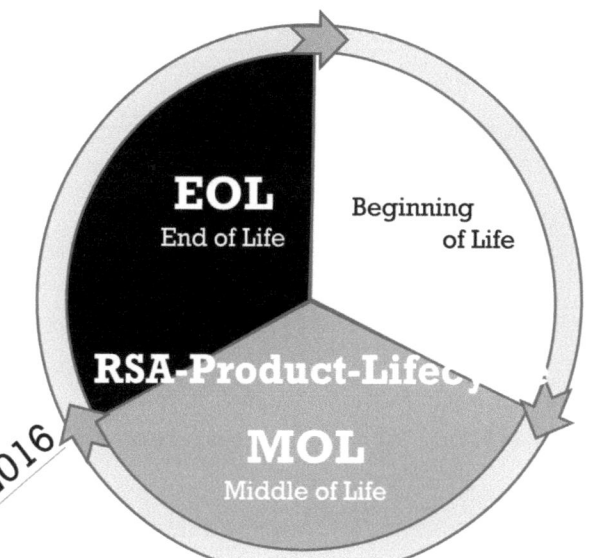

National Institute of Standards and Technology
U.S. Department of Commerce

- RSA is „no longer secure"...

- ECDSA is „no longer secure"...

- McEliece & NTRU seem to be successors...

- Why is media not discussing it in detail?...

- What happens with RSA-Online-Banking?...

- How can Messengers integrate McEliece-algorithm-code, or even get rid of RSA-algorithm-code?...

Cryptographic Algorithm	Type	Purpose	Impact from large-scale quantum computer
AES-256	Symmetric key	Encryption	Larger key sizes needed
SHA-256, SHA-3		Hash functions	Larger output needed
RSA	Public key	Signatures, key establishment	No longer secure
ECDSA, ECDH (Elliptic Curve Cryptography)	Public key	Signatures, key exchange	No longer secure
DSA (Finite Field Cryptography)	Public key	Signatures, key exchange	No longer secure

Table 1 - Impact of Quantum Computing on Common Cryptographic Algorithms

Source: NIST 2016

Ackermann & Klein: Caesura in Cryptography (2020)

53

BEGINNING OF A NEW LIFE-CYCLE: MCELIECE-ALGORITHM & NTRU-ALGORITHM

McEliece cryptosystem

- **McEliece** is an asymmetric encryption algorithm developed in 1978 by Robert McEliece.

- Using Goppa code / randomization in the encryption process.

- Post-Quantum cryptography: McEliece has resist cryptanalysis so far: Immune to attacks using Shor's algorithm.

- **McNoodle Library** provides an open source library for McEliece.

NTRUEncrypt & NTRUSign

- **NTRU** is an open source public-key cryptosystem that uses lattice-based cryptography.

- Unlike RSA and Elliptic Curve Cryptography, NTRU is not known to be vulnerable to quantum computer based attacks: Resistant to attacks using Shor's algorithm.

- Five open-source NTRU implementations exist today.

Shor's algorithm is a quantum computer algorithm for integer factorization: It solves the following problem: Given an integer N, find its prime factors.

Ackermann & Klein: Caesura in Cryptography (2020)

https://www.caltech.edu/about/news/robert-j-mceliece-19422019

THE MCELIECE ALGORITHM

- McNoodle is an open source library for the McEliece algorithm.

- Spot-On & Smoke Messenger integrate a classical McEliece implementation.

- The implementation is based on the software and writings of Antoon Bosselaers, René Govaerts, Robert McEliece, Bart Preneel, Marek Repka, Christopher Roering, Joos Vandewalle.

- Spot-On supports m value 11 and t value 51. For m = 11 and t = 51, k = 1487 and n = 2048. As a result, the message expansion factor is approximately 1.4. Parameters m = 12 and t = 68 are also provided.

- A private keys consists of matrices P-1 and S -1 , the code support L, a binary irreducible Goppa polynomial g, and a vector.

- The matrices contain 2048 x 2048 and 1487 x 1487 entries, respectively. The polynomial contains 51 entries. The vector contains 2048 entries. A total of 6,407,572 entries are required. As many as 12,873,361 bytes may be consumed by a private key.

- Approximately 74 MiB are required for housing six McEliece private keys.

- A public key consists of matrix $\hat{G}$ and t. A total of 1487 x 2048, or 3,045,376, entries are required. As many as 6,093,750 bytes are consumed.

- Included is an interpretation, model a, of the Fujisaki-Okamoto conversion. Please see https://www.emsec.rub.de/media/attachments/files/2013/03/mastersthesis-hudde-code-basedcryptography-library.pdf for more details. The key streams referenced in the aforementioned paper are generated via single-round PBKDF2 and SHA-256. The generated 32-byte salts are transferred as clear text.

- Also included is an interpretation, model b, of the Fujisaki-Okamoto conversion. Please see https://www.emsec.rub.de/media/attachments/files/2013/03/mastersthesis-hudde-code-basedcryptography-library.pdf for more details. The key streams referenced in the aforementioned paper are generated via SHAKE-256. libgcrypt 1.7.0 or newer is required.

Ackermann & Klein: Caesura in Cryptography (2020)

MCELIECE ENCRYPTION

- 1. Generate a random vector e of length n. The vector e will contain t randomly-dispersed ones.

- 2. Compute the SHA-256 digest of e || m, where m is the original message.

- 3. Apply the previously-computed digest to a single round of the PBKDF2 function. The generated key stream, k1, will contain 1488 bits of which the first 1487 will be consumed in the following computation. A 32-byte weakly-derived salt, s1, is provided to PBKDF2.

- 4. Compute $c1 = k1 * \hat{G} + e$.

- 5. Compute the SHA-256 digest of e.

- 6. Apply the previously-computed digest to a single round of the PBKDF2 function. The generated key stream, k2, will contain 1488 bits of which the first 1487 will be consumed in the following computation. A 32-byte weakly-derived salt, s2, is provided to PBKDF2.

- 7. Compute $c2 = k2$ xor m. 8. Transfer c1, c2, s1, and s2.

Ackermann & Klein: Caesura in Cryptography (2020)

MCELIECE DECRYPTION

- 1. Decrypt, via McEliece, c1 to obtain the original message m.

- 2. Compute the original error vector e via $e = c1 - m * \hat{G}$.

- 3. Compute the SHA-256 digest of e.

- 4. Apply the previously-computed digest to a single round of the PBKDF2 function. The generated key stream, k2, will contain 1488 bits of which the first 1487 will be consumed in the following computation. The 32-byte salt, s2, is provided to PBKDF2.

- 5. Compute mcar = c2 xor k2.

- 6. Compute the SHA-256 digest of e || mcar.

- 7. Apply the previously-computed digest to a single round of the PBKDF2 function. The generated key stream, k1, will contain 1488 bits of which the first 1487 will be consumed in the following computation. The 32-byte salt, s1, is provided to PBKDF2.

- 8. Verify that $c1 = k1 * \hat{G} + e$.

MCELIECE ALGORITHM APPLIED

- Spot-On Encryption Suite with McEliece.

- Smoke Crypto Chat Messenger known as worldwide the first open source mobile McEliece Messenger (3 Moduli).

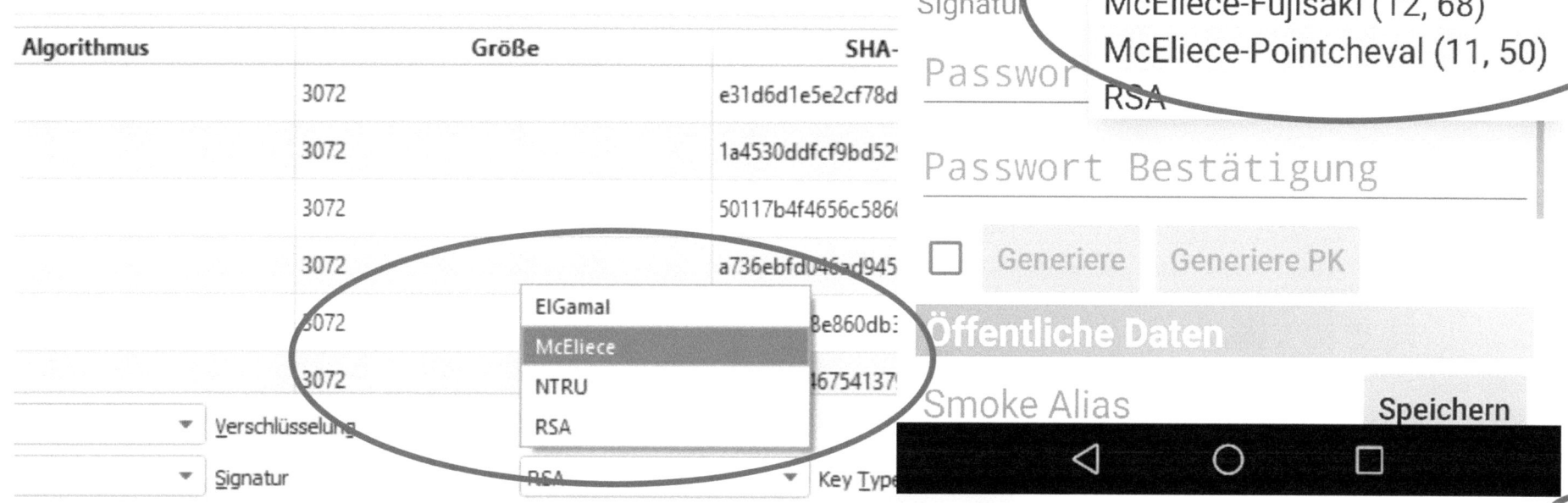

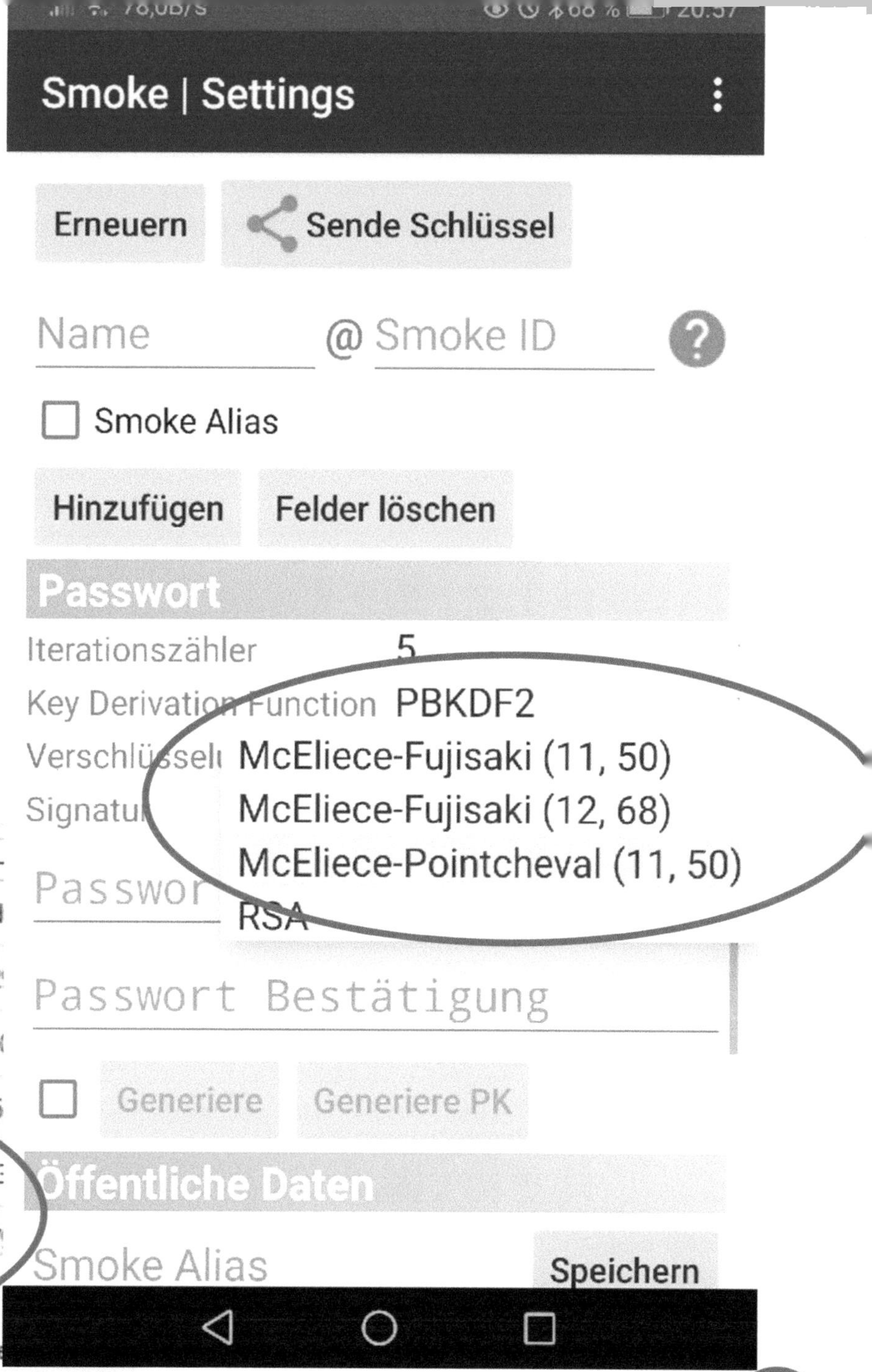

Ackermann & Klein: Caesura in Cryptography (2020)

hacking

QUANTUM COMPUTING

$\hat{z} = |0\rangle$

$\hat{z} = |0\rangle$

$|\psi\rangle$

θ

$\hat{y}$

ϕ

x

3x faster than 10-Min-Transrapid @MUC
watch?v=IchjVN_K7Fc

$-\hat{z} = |1\rangle$

$-\hat{z} = |1\rangle$

Post-quantum cryptography: To be secure against an attack by a quantum computer.

- 3 hard mathematical problems:
  - the integer factorization problem,
  - the discrete logarithm problem or
  - the elliptic-curve discrete logarithm problem.

  … can be easily solved on a powerful quantum computer running Shor's algorithm.

- McEliece & NTRU are still quantum-resistant.

- NASA & Google's **'Sycamore'** quantum computer was able to achieve "quantum supremacy" - solving a complex problem - in just three minutes and 20 seconds, compared to 10,000 years it would take the world's most advanced classical computer (Rieffel 2019 / Arute & Martinis 2019).

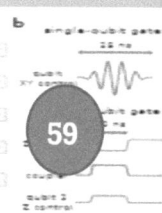

59

MACHINE LEARNING WITH CRYPTOGRAPHYIC TOKENS

- A security token is a physical device used to gain access to an electronically restricted resource.

- The token is used in addition to or in place of a password. It acts like an electronic key to access something.

- Examples include a wireless keycard opening a locked door, or in the case of a customer trying to access their bank account online, the use of a bank-provided token can prove that the customer is who they claim to be.

- Some tokens may store cryptographic keys, such as a digital signature, or biometric data, such as fingerprint details. Some may also store passwords.

- Tokenization, when applied to data security, is the process of substituting a sensitive data element with a non-sensitive equivalent, referred to as a token, that has no extrinsic or exploitable meaning or value.

- The token is a reference (i.e. identifier) that maps back to the sensitive data through a tokenization system.

- The software Spot-On Encryption Suite introduced Cryptographic Tokens as commands for servers within the Adaptive Echo (AE) Protocol.

APPLIED CRYPTOGRAPHY: FRAMEWORKS

Ackermann & Klein: Caesura in Cryptography (2020)

- Qt: (pronounced "cute") is a free and open-source widget toolkit for creating graphical user interfaces as well as cross-platform applications that run on various software and hardware platforms such as Linux, Windows, macOS, Android or embedded systems with little or no change in the underlying codebase while still being a native application with native capabilities and speed.

- Flutter: is an open-source UI software development kit. It is used to develop applications for Android, iOS, Linux, Mac, Windows, Google Fuchsia and the web from a single codebase. Flutter apps are written in the Dart language and make use of many of the language's more advanced features. On Windows, macOS and Linux Flutter runs in the Dart virtual machine which features a just-in-time execution engine. While writing and debugging an app, Flutter uses Just In Time compilation, allowing for "hot reload", with which modifications to source files can be injected into a running application. Flutter extends this with support for stateful hot reload, where in most cases changes to source code can be reflected immediately in the running app without requiring a restart or any loss of state. That is also for cryptographic security a to be researched field.

APPLIED CRYPTOGRAPHY: LIBRARIES

Bouncy Castle and Wolfcrypt are the only libraries for the NTRU algorithm, and McNoodle is currently the only library for the McEliece algorithm.

- **Libgcrypt:** Libgcrypt is a cryptography library developed as a separated module of GnuPG. It can also be used independently of GnuPG, but depends on its error-reporting library Libgpg-error. It provides functions for all fundamental cryptographic building blocks.

- **McNoodle:** McNoodle is an open source library for McEliece asymmetric encryption. The implementation is based on the PKC Calculator by Marek Repka. Other reference papers are in the source included. Divisions by zero may occur. (If this is a concern, please see mcnoodle_private_key::mcnoodle_private_key() and adjust the generator-discovery algorithm). The library has been tested on Debian AMD 64-bit, Debian ARM 32-bit, Debian PowerPC 32-bit, FreeBSD 32-bit, and Windows 7 with Cygwin. Repositories under: https://github.com/textbrowser/mcnoodle.

- **Bouncy Castle:** Bouncy Castle is a collection of APIs used in cryptography. It includes APIs for both the Java and the C# programming languages. The APIs are supported by a registered Australian charitable organization: Legion of the Bouncy Castle Inc.

- **Botan:** Botan is a BSD-licensed cryptographic and TLS library written in C++11. It provides a wide variety of cryptographic algorithms, formats, and protocols, e.g. SSL and TLS.

- **Crypto++:** Crypto++ is a free and open-source C++ class library of cryptographic algorithms and schemes. Crypto++ has been widely used in academia, student projects, open source and non-commercial projects, as well as businesses.

- **wolfCrypt:** wolfSSL is a small, portable, embedded SSL/TLS library targeted for use by embedded systems developers. It is an open source implementation of TLS written in C.

CRYPTOGRAPHY ON MOBILE DEVICES

- A mobile device (a handheld or wearable computer) can be   a smartphone, a robot or just an autonomous vehicle.

- Mobile devices are used by citizens to communicate…

  … and are fast enough to encrypt communications.

- Listening and spying: Smartphones are also used as instruments for interception and visual enlightenment through their cameras and microphones remotely controlled by hackers or the central owner of the operating system or by individual apps.

- A Trusted Execution Environment (TEE) is not given with many suppliers having access to the device or its parts.

- Try to buy a device with a Non-Google & Non-Apple operating system.

- Learn about & develop mobile communication apps including encryption.

e.g.
Cosmo Communicator
Smart Phone boots into
- Linux Phone Operating System,
- Sailfish OS,
- Android,
- UBPorts Ubuntu Touch for smart devices.

Ackermann & Klein: Caesura in Cryptography (2020)

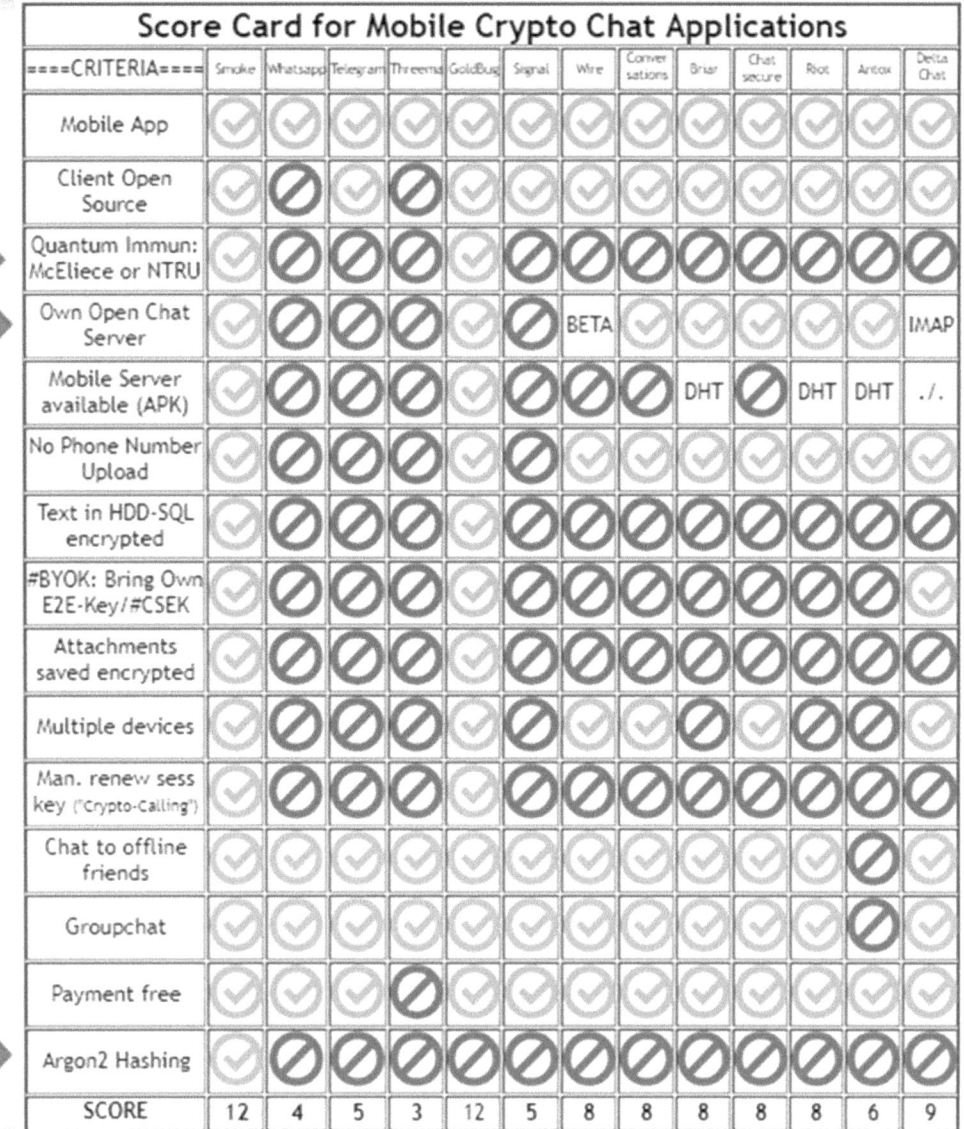

Score Card for Mobile Crypto Chat Applications

====CRITERIA====	Smoke	Whatsapp	Telegram	Threema	GoldBug	Signal	Wire	Conversations	Briar	Chat secure	Riot	Antox	Delta Chat
Mobile App	✓	✓	✓	✓	✓	✓	✓	✓	✓	✓	✓	✓	✓
Client Open Source	✓	⊘	✓	⊘	✓	✓	✓	✓	✓	✓	✓	✓	✓
Quantum Immun: McEliece or NTRU	✓	⊘	⊘	⊘	✓	⊘	⊘	⊘	⊘	⊘	⊘	⊘	⊘
Own Open Chat Server	✓	⊘	⊘	⊘	✓	⊘	BETA	✓	✓	✓	✓	✓	IMAP
Mobile Server available (APK)	✓	⊘	⊘	✓	⊘	⊘	⊘	DHT	⊘	DHT	DHT		./.
No Phone Number Upload	✓	⊘	⊘	⊘	✓	⊘	✓	✓	✓	✓	✓	✓	✓
Text in HDD-SQL encrypted	✓	⊘	⊘	⊘	✓	⊘	⊘	⊘	⊘	⊘	⊘	⊘	⊘
#BYOK: Bring Own E2E-Key/#CSEK	✓	⊘	⊘	✓	✓	⊘	⊘	⊘	⊘	⊘	⊘	⊘	✓
Attachments saved encrypted	✓	⊘	⊘	⊘	✓	⊘	⊘	⊘	⊘	⊘	⊘	⊘	⊘
Multiple devices	✓	⊘	⊘	⊘	✓	⊘	✓	✓	✓	⊘	⊘	⊘	✓
Man. renew sess key ("Crypto-Calling")	✓	⊘	⊘	⊘	✓	⊘	⊘	⊘	⊘	⊘	⊘	⊘	⊘
Chat to offline friends	✓	✓	✓	✓	✓	✓	✓	✓	✓	✓	✓	⊘	✓
Groupchat	✓	✓	✓	✓	✓	✓	✓	✓	✓	✓	✓	⊘	✓
Payment free	✓	✓	✓	⊘	✓	✓	✓	✓	✓	✓	✓	✓	✓
Argon2 Hashing	✓	⊘	⊘	⊘	⊘	⊘	⊘	⊘	⊘	⊘	⊘	⊘	⊘
SCORE	12	4	5	3	12	5	8	8	8	8	8	6	9

MESSAGING APPS WITH CRYPTOGRAPHY ON MOBILE DEVICES

„The easy to install open source chat **server software** is more important than the graphical user interface of the messenger App client.“

Source: Internet

Ackermann & Klein: Caesura in Cryptography (2020)

CRYPTOGRAPHY ON MOBILE DEVICES: e.g. SMOKE CRYPTO CHAT & DELTA CHAT

Smoke Crypto Chat

- Own Crypto Chat Server: SmokeStack for Android = independent of third party (IMAP) server providers.

- AutoCrypt. SomokeStack Server serves additionally as Key Server for AutoCrypt

- Offline-Messaging over „Ozone"-Postboxes.

- Quantum-resistant with McEliece Algorithm (3 Moduli).

- Fiasco Forwarding with Fiasco Keys

- Cryptographic Calling: #BYOK: (Define &) Bring your own (session) key.

- Smoke-ID (based on SipHash) (or over Aliase) for easy key transfer:

- No phone number usage/upload/sharing.

- For Developers: Easy to compile due to less dependency on third libraries.

Delta-Chat since 2016

- Based on POPTASTIC Protocol 2015 (Encrypted Chat over E-Mail Servers)

- Based on IMAP Servers = depending on E-Mail-Providers allowing this App.

- Offline-Messaging over „IMAP"-Postboxes.

- Based on OpenPGP (RSA & ECDSA) = not Quantum-immun.

- No Cryptographic Calling.

- No Session Key renewal.

- Implemented Repleo & EPKS as AutoCrypt.

- No phone number usage/upload/sharing.

- For Developers: Difficult to compile due to higher dependency on libraries (c++/Rust kernel with java gui, etc.)

- Excellent GUI.

Source: https://momedo.github.io/momedo/

Ackermann & Klein: Caesura in Cryptography (2020)

SMOKE

- Smoke is an encrypting mobile Chat Messenger, which is
  - open source (for client <u>and</u> server),
  - quantum-computing secure with the also applied McEliece algorithm next to RSA with key-sizes above standard,
  - allows you to use your own decentral chat server,
  - does not send your phone number to central servers or new contacts,
  - and further, is able to define your own end-to-end passwords manually by your individual choice (or by Cryptographic Calling).

- If locked, all is encrypted and, also attachments are saved on the hard disk only encrypted.

- Some reviewers regard Smoke as worldwide the first mobile secure McEliece Messenger (3 Moduli).

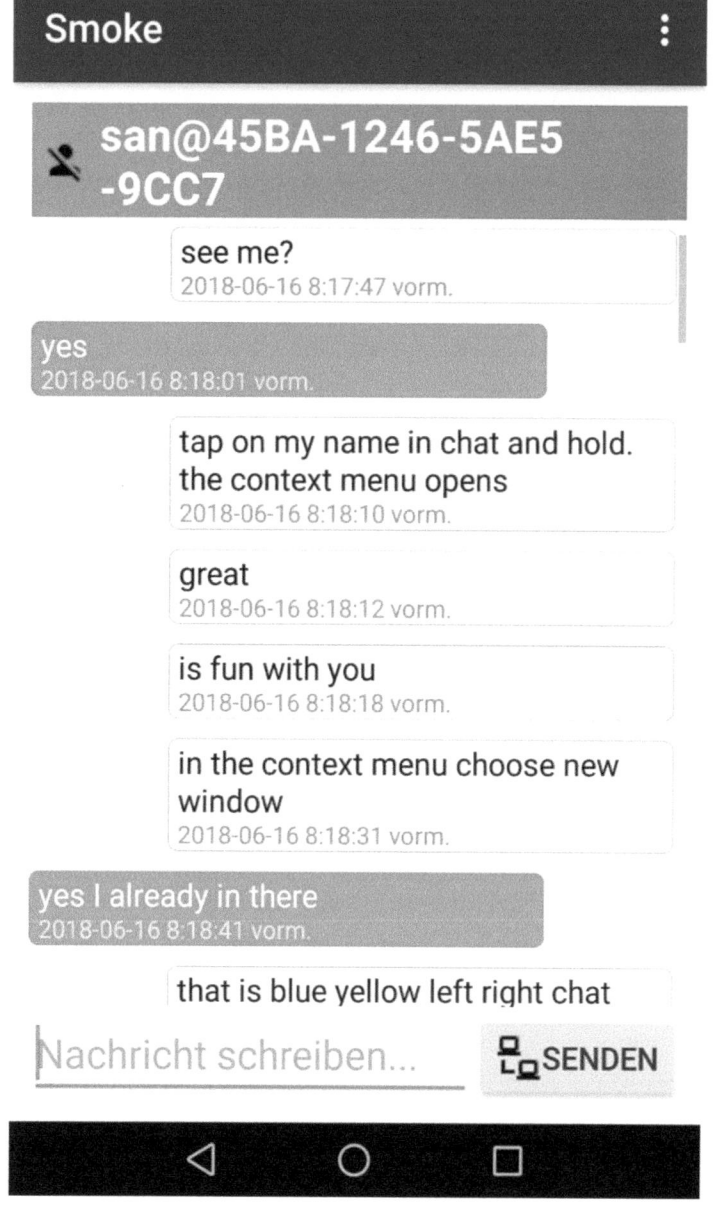

Ackermann & Klein: Caesura in Cryptography (2020)

POPTASTIC: ENCRYPTED CHAT OVER E-MAIL-SERVERS

- POPTASTIC is a function, which enables encrypted chat and encrypted e-mail over the regular POP3 and IMAP-Postboxes of a user.

- Implemented within the Spot-On Encryption Suite, it recognizes automatically, if the message has to be regarded as a chat-message or as an e-mail-message.

- For that, the POPTASTIC encryption key is used. Once with a friend exchanged, this key is sending all e-mails between two e-mail-partners only as encrypted e-mail.

- Third, POPTASTIC enables – respective the insertion of the POP3 / IMAP account information into the settings – also an old-fashioned and unencrypted E-mail-communication to @-E-mail-Addresses.

- Spot-On extends the Instant Messaging with this function to a regular e-mail-client and also to an always encrypting e-mail-client over the POPTASTIC Key.

- The e-mail-addresses for encrypted e-mails are indicated with a lock icon.

- Encrypted Chat is enabled over the free ports for e-mail also behind more restrictive hardware environments at any time.
- A mobile implementation of POPTASTIC is given by DeltaChat (smartphones) and GoldBug Crypto Chat Messenger (Win 10 tablets).

DELTA CHAT

- Delta.Chat is a Chat Messenger since late 2016 over e-mail servers implementing the prior released POPTASTIC (POP3/IMAP) Protocol idea (since 2014 released, see also Edwards, ibid): here over IMAP and OpenPGP.

- Delta Chat has no own servers, but uses the most massive and diverse open messaging system ever: the existing e-mail server network. That's POPTASTIC.

- Encrypted chat with anyone, if one knows the e-mail address.

- Delta Chat is an emerging Chat App (since 2016, and since 2019 in beta status) that uses e-mails for transfering messages and encrypts the chat between two Delta-Chat installations.

- Key transport is done via the EPKS/Repleo derivation AutoCrypt.

- Some e-mail-Providers like outlook.com, hotmail.com, office365.com have not continued since 2019-02 to fix technical issues with Delta Chat (Issue #561).

- The hybrid implementation of additional private servers seems to be an adequate solution for that development of lacking support and limits of file sharing perspectives over e-mail servers at the same time.

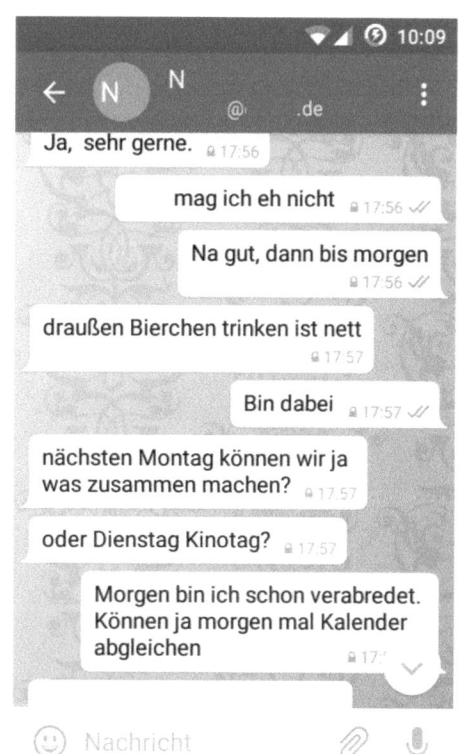

POPTASTIC II:
FILE-SHARING & TURTLE HOPPING OVER POPTASTIC

- "Turtle File Sharing" Hopping (as known from RetroShare, comp. Tanenbaum et al. 2004) over a friend-to-friend Web-of-Trust of e-mail-users as suggested by Gasakis/Schmidt (2018:67) under the concept of "POPTASTIC Echo Turtle" for an extension of the POPTASTIC Protocol respective an POPTASTIC Network is currently not yet implemented in Delta Chat.

- it would open up a secure file searching and sharing network over mobile devices between trusted friends the music/copyright-industry cannot influence as long as encryption and e-mail-servers exist for to be sent attachments (e.g. mp3s) over certain hops of a graph-route: e.g. a query-hit-sender and a searching receiver would share an ephemeral-temp public key over the POPTASTIC Protocol via E-Mail from friend to friend with some routing information and then would wrap the MP3-file with their exchanged asymmetric encryption and send it over the same graph:

- Such a POPTASTIC 2 Protocol would provide AutoCrypt-Transportation of the key and AutoSend-Transportation of the MP3-File. Data from a Queryhit-Node is turtle-hopping over the e-mail-boxes of several friends to the searching friend.

- While utilizing a POPTASTIC Network for file sharing it must be spoken of routing, while utilizing an Echo Network (e.g. over the Mobile Crypto Chat App Smoke Messenger) it would be "beyond cryptographic routing" (ibid).

XMPP: CONVERSATIONS CLIENT

- Conversations is a free instant messaging client for Android. It supports the exchange of encrypted text and picture messages.

- OMEMO-encrypted: OMEMO is an extension to the Extensible Messaging and Presence Protocol (XMPP, "Jabber") for multi-client end-to-end encryption. It is an open standard based on the Double Ratchet Algorithm and the Personal Eventing Protocol (PEP, XEP-0163).

- based on the Double Ratchet (means the key for the next message is placed in a history message): once known one key, the encryption is "ribbling off" under permanent record.

- XMPP created a Manifest to implement encryption. Just a few clients did and just two servers can operate: ejabbered and Prosody.

- Servers are not handling Key Management

- The Encryption of Omemo is still based on the algorithm, not being quantum secure. Curve25519/Ed25519

- Still an algorithm like McEliece or NTRU is missing.

ENCRYPTED GROUP CHAT
E.G. WITH GOLDBUG MESSENGER

Secure Chat Messenger & E-Mail Client with
Multi-Encryption http://goldbug.SF.net -
Research-Project GUI & App for @spotonsfnet
Kernels - A McEliece Messenger

- BUZZ Chat is a Group Chat based on AES-256

- URL: Magnet URI Standard with Cryptographic
  Values (or Tokens):

- magnet:?
  rn=Developer_Channel_Key
  &xf=10000&xs=Developer_Channel_Salt
  &ct=aes256
  &hk=Developer_Channel_Hash_Key
  &ht=sha384
  &xt=urn:buzz

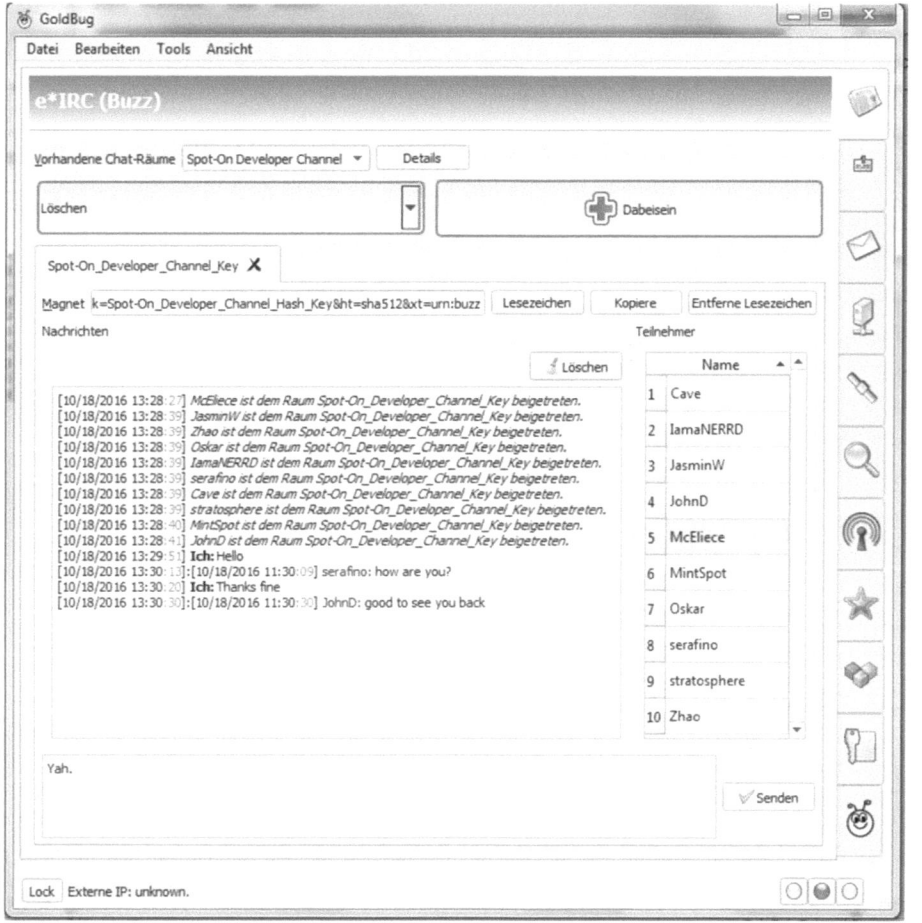

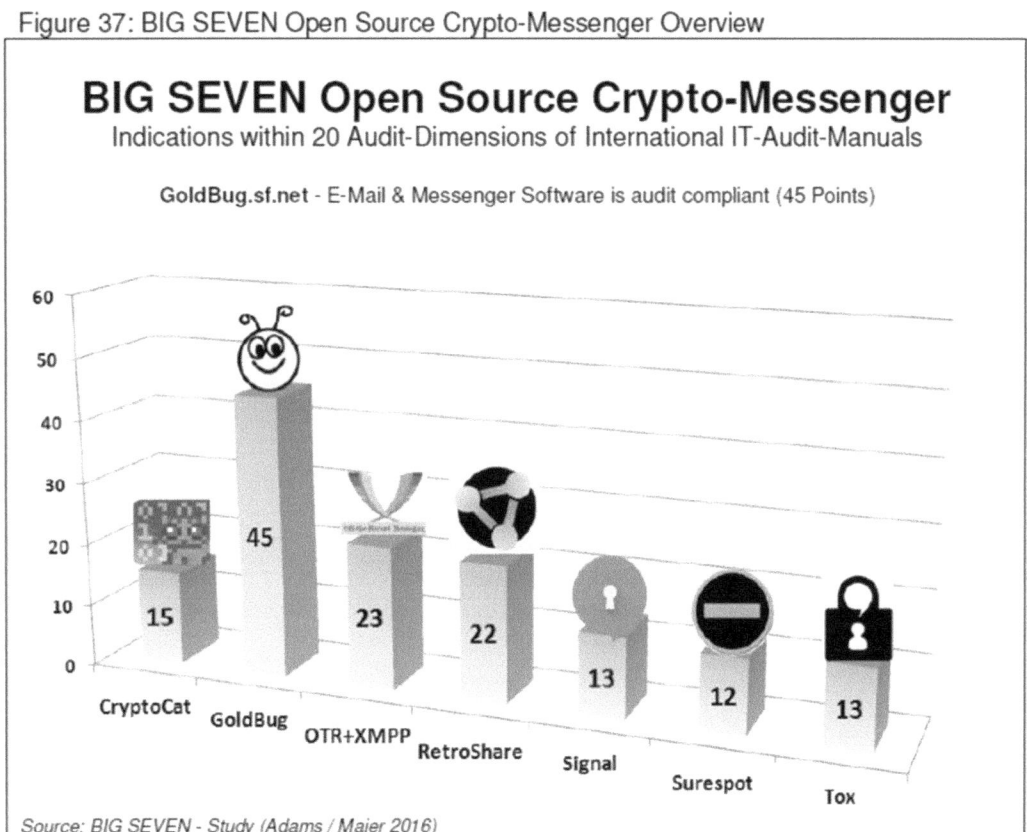

BIG SEVEN Open Source Crypto-Messenger

Indications within 20 Audit-Dimensions of International IT-Audit-Manuals

GoldBug.sf.net - E-Mail & Messenger Software is audit compliant (45 Points)

Source: BIG SEVEN - Study (Adams / Maier 2016)

MESSENGER SCORECARDS: FURTHER DESKTOP CLIENTS

BIG SEVEN STUDY 2016

BIG SEVEN STUDY 2016

7 open source Crypto-Messengers to be compared

or: Comprehensive Confidentiality Review & Audit
of GoldBug Encrypting E-Mail-Client & Secure Instant Messenger

by David Adams & Ann-Kathrin Maier

English & Deutsch. Reprint.

Adams/Maier (2016): ISBN 9783750408975.

10 TRENDS IN CRYPTO MESSAGING

- 01: Consolidation of E-Mail & Chat.
- 02: Data Storage encrypted on HDD.
- 03: Zero Knowledge: SMP & Juggernaut.
- 04: Multi-Encryption.
- 05: Easy Server Setup with Key-Sharing.
- 06: Instant Perfect Forward Secrecy (IPFS).
- 07: Individual Choice of Crypto-DNA-Values.
- 08: E2E Encryption: Manual Key Definition for Cryptographic Calling.
- 09: Avoidance of Recording of Metadata.
- 10: Quantum Immunity with McEliece & NTRU.

Source: Adams/Maier: Big 7 Crypto Study (2016)

Ackermann & Klein: Caesura in Cryptography (2020)

10 Trends in **Crypto Messaging**

A Study on the open source Applications GoldBug, CryptoCat, OTR+XMPP, RetroShare, Signal, Surespot and Tox.

Adams, D. / Maier, A.K. (2016)

INSTALLING AN OWN CRYPTO CHAT SERVER

Chat Server differ for the easyness of a set-up and administration.
The highlighted ones deny plaintext or can handle video streams.

- BigBlueButton Chat Server (not e2e encrypted).

- GoldBug Chat Server.

- IMAP Chat Server.

- Jitsi Chat Server (not e2e encrypted).

- Matrix Chat Server.

- OwnCloud Chat Server (not e2e encrypted).

- Signal Chat Server.

- SmokeStack Chat Server (Android Server).

- Spot-On Chat Server.

- Spot-On Lite Chat Server (Haedless Linux Server).

- Prosody/Ejabbered Chat Server.

- Wire Chat Server (no source for pre-built AWS Docker Cloud available).

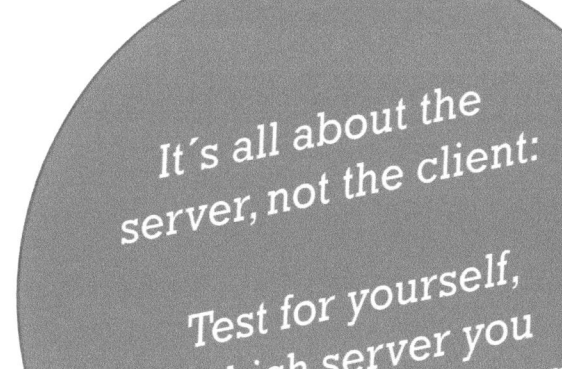

It´s all about the server, not the client:

Test for yourself, which server you can set up your own without hassle?

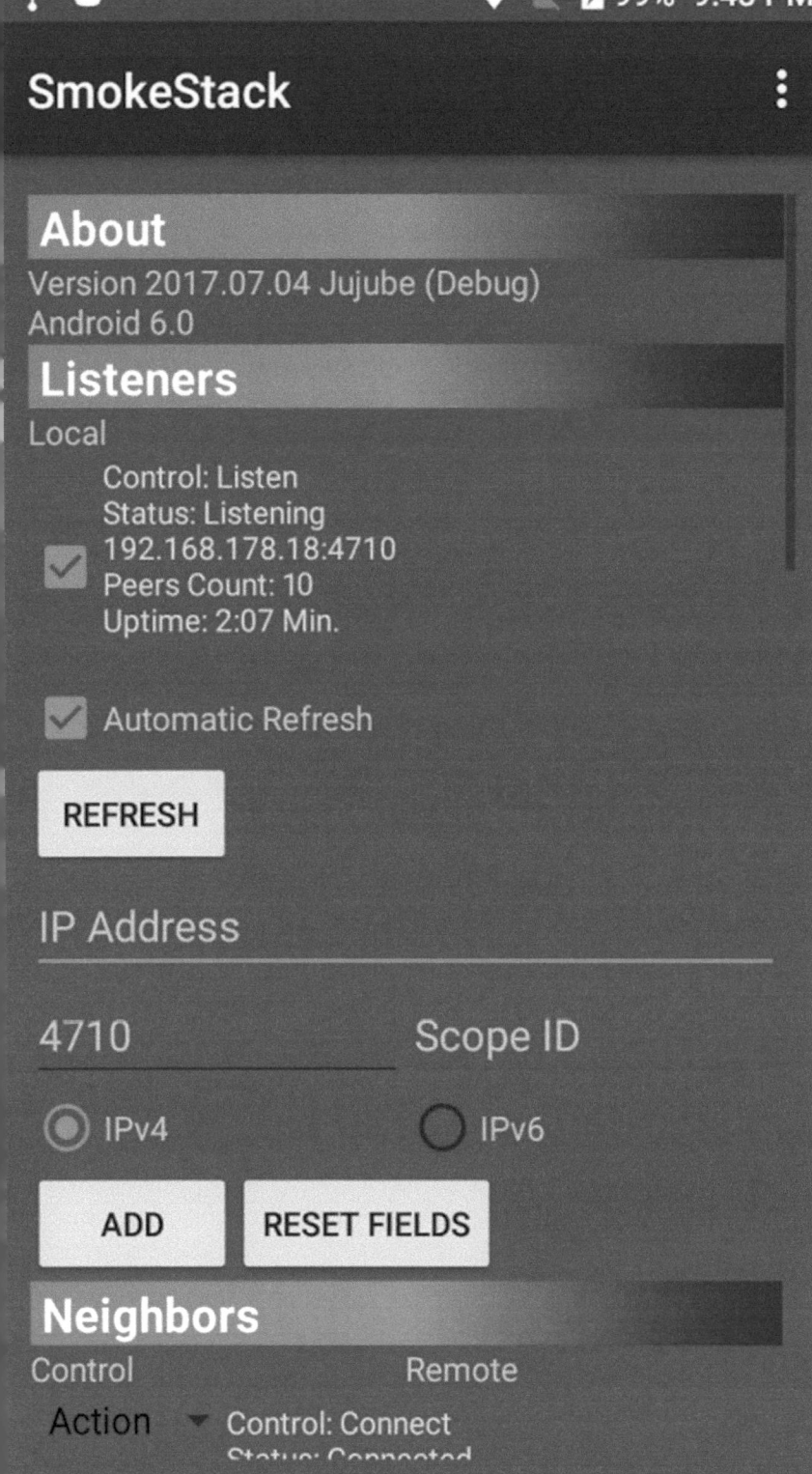

EXERCISE: SMOKESTACK CRYPTO CHAT SERVER INSTALLATION

SmokeStack is known as the first Chat Server for Android

- handling encryption

- and McEliece Ciphertext.

- Easy to set up.

- Easy in administration.

- Ready for each Android device in your pocket.

- Provides Ozone Post-Boxes for Messaging to Offline Friends.

- Compatible with Smoke Crypto Chat Client, Spot-On Encryption Suite Chat and GoldBug Client.

- Try to set up a Stack on an Android device and connect a Smoke Chat Client from another Android device to it.

EXERCISE: CHAT-SERVER SOFTWARE COMPARISON

Please find criteria to compare server software and complete such a table.

	SmokeStack Server	Matrix Server	Spot-On Lite Server	Signal Server
Easy to install.	☑			
Easy to administer.	☑	☑	☑	
Provides a Key Management.	☑		☑	
Is open source.	☑	☑	☑	
Has an installation tutorial within this school/university.				
Is well documented.				
Easy to compile from source.				
....				

KEY MANAGEMENT

- Key management refers to management of cryptographic keys in a cryptosystem. This includes dealing with the generation, exchange, storage, use, crypto-shredding (destruction) and replacement of keys. It includes cryptographic protocol design, key servers, user procedures, and other relevant protocols.

- Successful key management is critical to the security of a cryptosystem.

- A public key infrastructure (PKI) is a set of roles, policies, hardware, software and procedures needed to create, manage, distribute, use, store and revoke digital certificates and manage public-key encryption.

- A PKI is an arrangement that binds public keys with respective identities of entities (like people and organizations). The binding is established through a process of registration and issuance of certificates at and by a certificate authority (CA).

- The server SmokeStack for encrypted Chat has implemented a Key management. This communication server also serves as a private public-key server. A SmokeStack administrator is responsible for coordinating the storage of public-key pairs of participants. Participants may request public-key pairs of specific participants via their Ozone Postbox-addresses within the server.

- Decentralized Identifiers (DIDs) eliminates dependence on centralized registries for identifiers as well as centralized certificate authorities for key management. This architecture is referred to as decentralized PKI (DPKI).

- As Ozone storage options are decentralized redundant, the realized quasi-decentralized PKI within that server is a good practice model for that decentralized identifiers (DID) approach.

SEARCHABLE ENCRYPTION:
E.G. SEARCH WITHIN ENCRYPTED DATABASES

Database encryption can generally be defined as a process that uses an algorithm to transform data stored in a database into "cipher text" that is incomprehensible without first being decrypted. It can therefore be said that the purpose of database encryption is to protect the data stored in a database from being accessed by individuals.

- **Symmetric database encryption:** Symmetric encryption in the context of database encryption involves a private key being applied to data that is stored and called from a database. This private key alters the data in a way that causes it to be unreadable without first being decrypted. Data is encrypted when saved, and decrypted when opened given that the user knows the private key.

- **Asymmetric database encryption:** Asymmetric encryption expands on symmetric encryption by incorporating two different types of keys into the encryption method: private and public keys. A public key can be accessed by anyone and is unique to one user whereas a private key is a secret key that is unique to and only known by one user. In most scenarios the public key is the encryption key whereas the private key is the decryption key. As an example, if individual A would like to send a message to individual B using asymmetric encryption, he would encrypt the message using Individual B's public key and then send the encrypted version. Individual B would then be able to decrypt the message using his private key. Individual C would not be able to decrypt Individual A's message, as Individual C's private key is not the same as Individual B's private key.

Spot-On Encryption Suite provides a model to search URLs in an encrypted database.

Alves, Pedro G. M. R. / Aranha, Diego F.: A framework for searching encrypted databases, Journal of Internet Services and Applications, December 2018, 9:1: URL: https://link.springer.com/article/10.1186/s13174-017-0073-0

Ackermann & Klein: Caesura in Cryptography (2020)

SPECIFIC TOOLS FOR ENCRYPTION

ENCRYPTION OF THE OPERATING SYSTEM/HDD VERACRYPT & LINUX CRYPT & DISCCRYPTOR

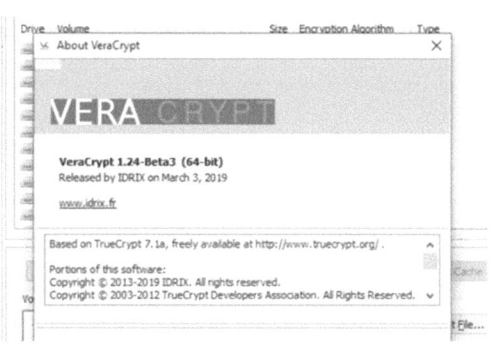

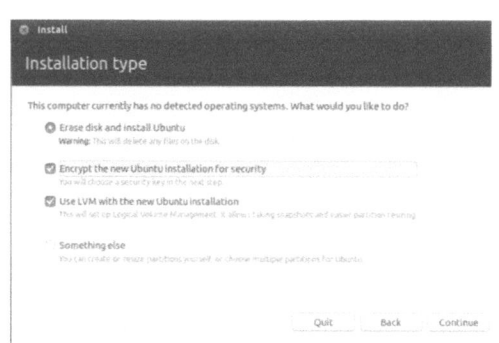

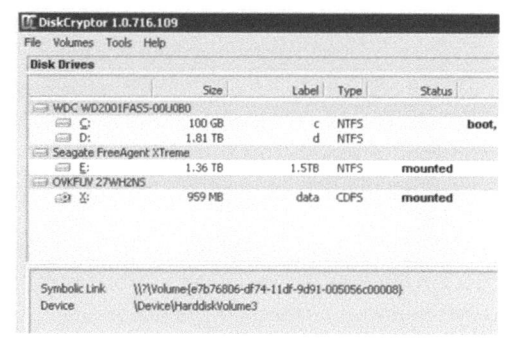

- VeraCrypt (was: TrueCrypt) is a source-available freeware utility used for on-the-fly encryption (OTFE). It can create a virtual encrypted disk within a file or encrypt a partition or (in Windows) the entire storage device with pre-boot authentication.

- https://www.veracrypt.fr/

- Most Linux distributions make it easy to encrypt home folders or even entire partitions. For Linux users, LUKS is based on cryptsetup and uses dm-crypt as the disk encryption backend. Short for Linux Unified Key Setup, LUKS specifies a platform-independent standard on-disk format.

- https://help.ubuntu.com/community/Full_Disk_Encryption_Howto_2019

- DiskCryptor supports FAT12, FAT16, FAT32, NTFS and exFAT file systems. DiskCryptor supports any Microsoft operation system since Windows 2000. Other operation systems (like Linux, etc.) are currently not supported.

- https://www.diskcryptor.org/

DATA & FILES
HARD DISC ENCRYPTION VERACRYPT

- VeraCrypt is a source-available freeware utility used for on-the-fly encryption (OTFE). It can create a virtual encrypted disk within a file or encrypt a partition or (in Windows) the entire storage device with pre-boot authentication.

- VeraCrypt is a fork of the discontinued TrueCrypt project. Many security improvements have been implemented and issues raised by TrueCrypt code audits have been fixed. VeraCrypt includes optimized implementations of cryptographic hash functions and ciphers which boost performance on CPUs.

- As with its predecessor TrueCrypt, VeraCrypt supports plausible deniability by allowing a single "hidden volume" to be created within another volume. In addition, the Windows versions of VeraCrypt have the ability to create and run a hidden encrypted operating system whose existence may be denied.

Ackermann & Klein: Caesura in Cryptography (2020)

HARD DISC ENCRYPTION VERACRYPT

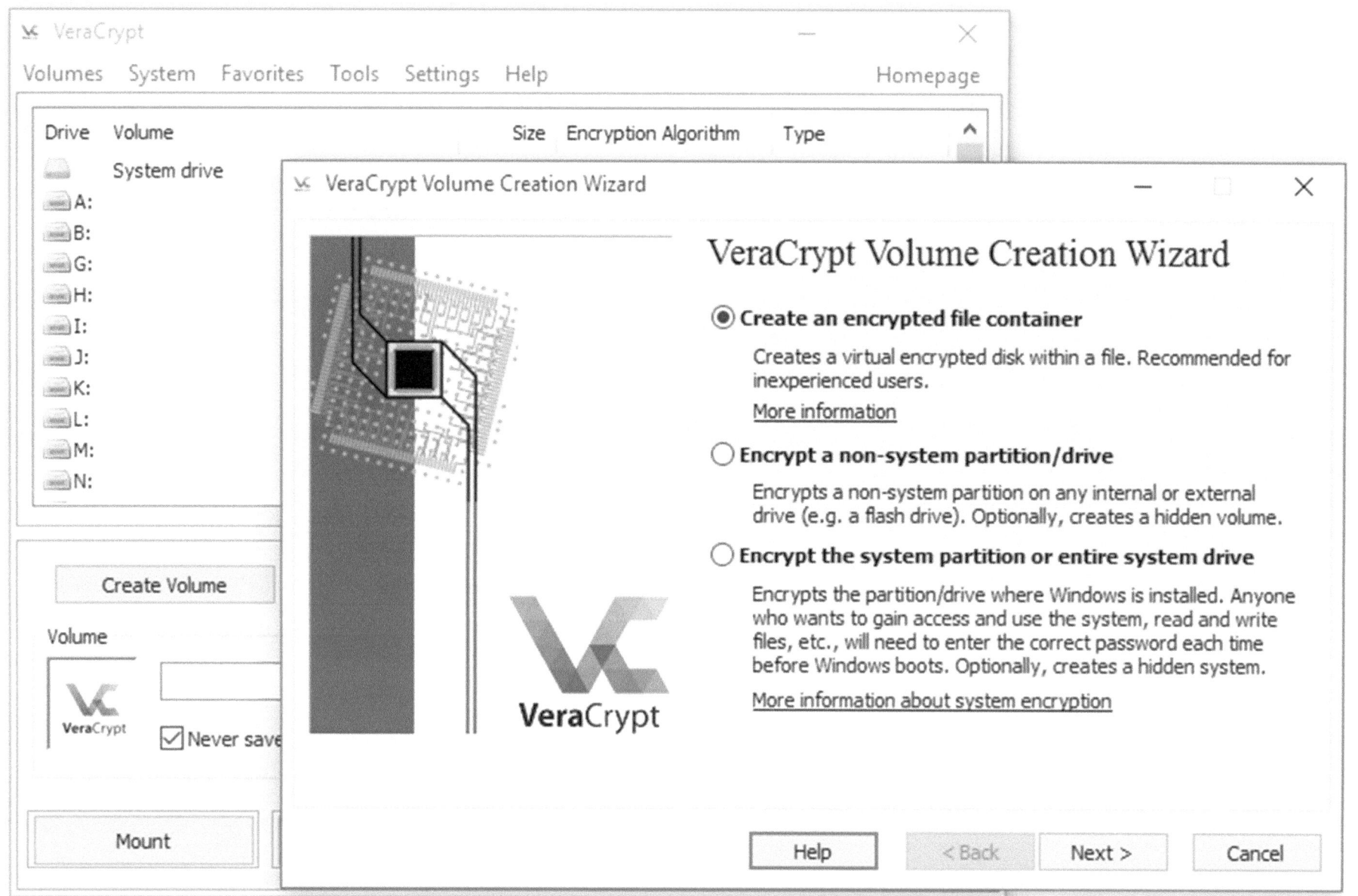

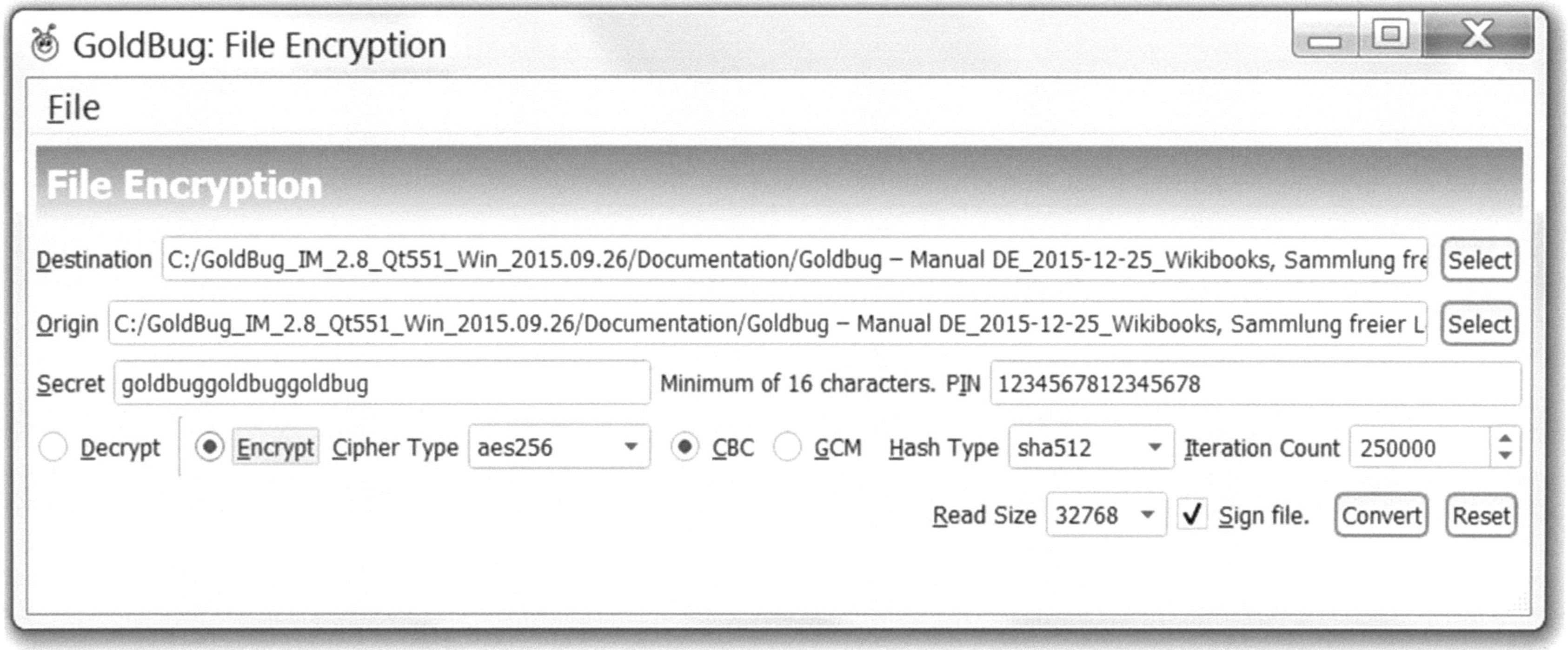

GoldBug: File Encryption

File

File Encryption

Destination | C:/GoldBug_IM_2.8_Qt551_Win_2015.09.26/Documentation/Goldbug – Manual DE_2015-12-25_Wikibooks, Sammlung fre | [Select]

Origin | C:/GoldBug_IM_2.8_Qt551_Win_2015.09.26/Documentation/Goldbug – Manual DE_2015-12-25_Wikibooks, Sammlung freier L | [Select]

Secret | goldbuggoldbuggoldbug | Minimum of 16 characters. PIN | 1234567812345678

○ Decrypt ● Encrypt Cipher Type | aes256 ▼ ● CBC ○ GCM Hash Type | sha512 ▼ Iteration Count | 250000 ⇕

Read Size | 32768 ▼ ✓ Sign file. [Convert] [Reset]

http://goldbug.sf.net/

FILE ENCRYPTION:
GOLDBUG & CRYPTOMATOR

https://cryptomator.org/

SPOT-ON ENCRYPTION SUITE

Spot-On Encryption Suite is a
- secure instant chat messenger and
- encrypting e-mail client

that also includes additional features such as
- group chat,
- file transfer, and a
- URL search based on an implemented URL database,
which can be peer-to-peer connected to other
nodes.

Thus, the three basic functions frequently used by a regular Internet user in the Internet - communication (chat / email), web search and file transfer - are represented in an encrypted environment safely and comprehensively.

It can be spoken from Spot-On as of an encryption suite. It might be regarded as the most elaborated, up-to-date and diversificated encryption software currently.

Explored at universities and schools for learning and training of applied cryptography and for study of cryptographic processes within tutorials.

The three S: Speaking (by text), Searching and Sending – are now secure over the Internet within one software suite: Open source for everyone!

Ackermann & Klein: Caesura in Cryptography (2020)

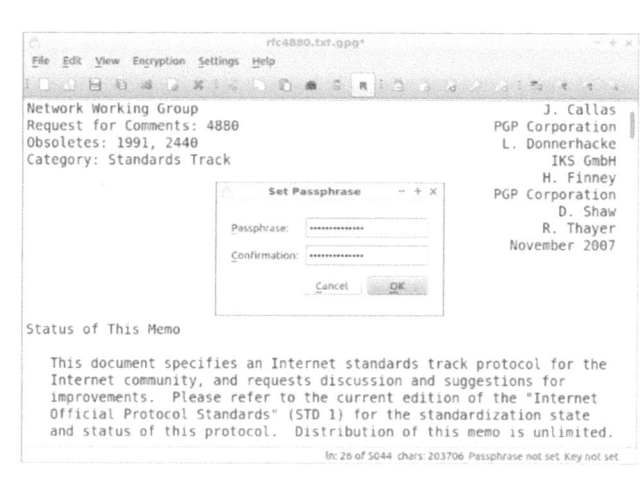

TEXT ENCRYPTION PADS E.G. ROSETTA CRYPTOPAD

- Conversion Pad

- within the Encryption Suite Spot-On

- Encrypts text with symmetric keys

- Name is from Rosetta Stone:

- https://en.wikipedia.org/wiki/Rosetta_Stone

https://textbrowser.github.io/spot-on/
since 2013

https://github.com/evpo/EncryptPad
Initial commit on 21 Feb 2016

PASSWORD/PASSPHRASE CREATION & SECURITY

- As a Password will be hashed – more important than the complexity of a password is to enter it not on a taped device.

- Keyboard Apps on Android or Android itself might be taped and sending text to home.

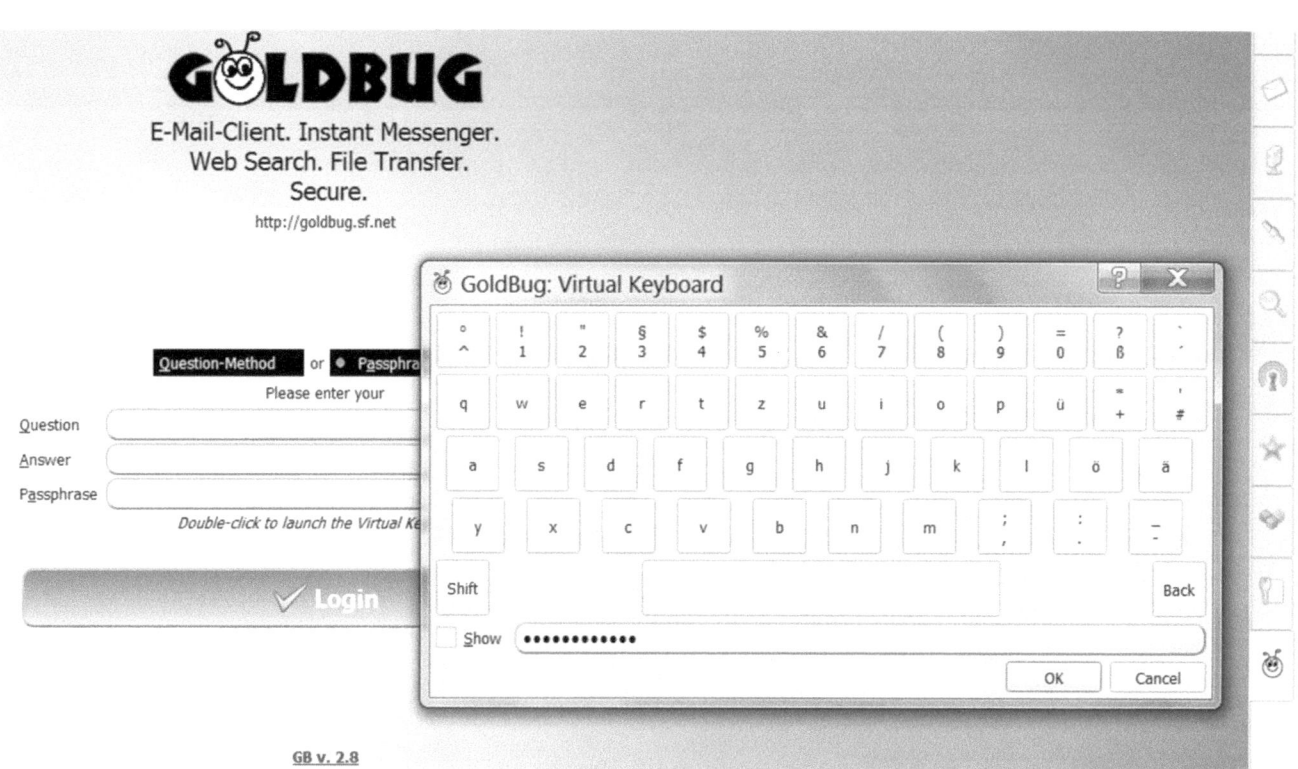

- Try a Trusted Excecution Environment (TEE).

- Try an App with Exit button, that closes all encrypted storage containers.

- E.g. GoldBug provides with a double click in the login field a virtual keyboard, so that only mouseclicks are recordable.

DOOBLE WEB BROWSER & SW-IRON

- All Data is saved **encrypted** in Dooble.

- Dooble Web browser is a free and open-source Web browser that was created to improve privacy. Currently, Dooble is available for FreeBSD, Linux, OS X, OS/2, and Windows. Dooble uses Qt for its user interface and abstraction from the operating system and processor architecture. As a result, Dooble should be portable to any system that supports OpenSSL, POSIX threads, Qt, SQLite, and other libraries.

- Dooble has been announced as one of the top five best secure browsers. PCWorld reviews Dooble on the feature side as "rendering quickly, even on image-heavy sites". The Guardian recommends Dooble as an alternative browser against surveillance: "Try out a privacy-focused browser such as Dooble." Dooble further has been rated as the ninth of ten "top" Linux browsers by Jack Wallen.

- SRWare Iron is a Chromium-based web browser developed by the German company SRWare. It primarily aims to eliminate usage tracking and other privacy-compromising functionality that the Google Chrome browser includes. Iron ships with certain Chromium privacy options switched on by default, it provides some additional features that distinguish it from Google Chrome.

- The following main Google Chrome features is not present in Iron: RLZ identifier, an encoded string sent together with all queries to Google.

- No Browsing Data is sent to Google based on RLZ identifier.

- (Cookies can be used instead. Dooble Web Browser provides a "Cookie Washer").

https://www.unixmen.com/dooble-a-web-browser-specially-designed-for-security-and-privacy/
https://blog.chromium.org/2008/10/google-chrome-chromium-and-google.html

RETROSHARE & ALLIANCE P2P

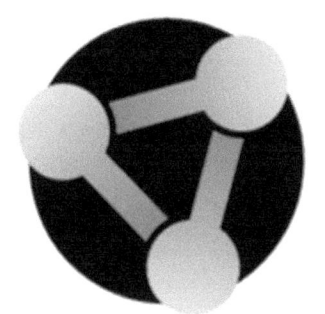

- Retroshare is a free and open-source peer-to-peer communication and file sharing app based on a friend-to-friend network built on GNU Privacy Guard (GPG). Optionally, peers may communicate certificates and IP addresses from and to their friends.

- It is important to remember that while Retroshare's encryption makes it virtually impossible for an ISP or another external observer to know what one is downloading or uploading, this limitation does not apply to members of the user's Retroshare circle and web of trust.

- https://github.com/RetroShare

- Alliance is a private and secure environment to communicate and share files with people you know. Hence, Alliance is a friend-to-friend network.

- It is written in Java 5.0 using Swing and asynchronous IO (java.nio package). The current implementation uses TCP/IP. Encryption is a vital part of Alliance. Encryption uses the SSL package in Java 5.0 (SSLEngine class).

- http://alliancep2p.sf.net/

Ackermann & Klein: Caesura in Cryptography (2020)

ENCRYPTED P2P DATA STORAGE: OFFSYSTEM/OFFLOAD & FREENET

- The Owner-Free File System (OFF System, or OFFload for short) is a peer-to-peer distributed file system in which all shared files are represented by randomized multi-used data blocks. Instead of anonymizing the network, the data blocks are anonymized and therefore, only data garbage is ever exchanged and stored and no forwarding via intermediate nodes is required. The block-recover information is neither exchanged encrypted nor among friends in a web-of-trust.

- Freenet is a peer-to-peer platform for censorship-resistant communication. It uses a decentralized distributed data store to keep and deliver information, and has a suite of free software for publishing and communicating on the Web without fear of censorship. Freenet added a web-of-trust as option to exchange blocks and recover-links only with friends - and not with peers.

http://offload.sourceforge.net/ & http://offsystem.sourceforge.net/

https://freenetproject.org/

Ackermann & Klein: Caesura in Cryptography (2020)

P2P E-MAIL
SPOT-ON EMAIL & OZONE POSTBOXES & BITMESSAGE

- BitMessage is a decentralized, encrypted, peer-to-peer, trustless communications protocol that can be used by one person to send encrypted messages to another person, or to multiple subscribers. BitMessage gained a reputation for being out of reach of warrantless wiretapping due to the decentralized nature of the protocol, and its encryption being difficult to crack.

E-Mail-Clients for the Echo-Network provide four new Methods of p2p/decentral and encrypted E-Mail next to BitMessage with the following protocols:

- E-Mail Institutions (Spot-On-E-Mail)

- E-Mail-Storage in a third Friend (Spot-On-E-Mail)

- POPTASTIC-E-Mail Encryption

- Ozone Postboxes (Smoke Messenger)

Source: Nomenclatura Encyclopaedia 2019

ENCRYPTED ALTERNATIVES TO IMAP? NEW (P2P) E-MAIL POSTBOXES

- IMAP

- POPTASTIC

- Spot-On cryptographic E-Mail

- E-Mail Institutions

- E-Mail Storage in a common Friend/Buddy/private Server

- P2P-Email

- Ozone-Postboxes with SmokeStack symmetric redundnacy.

E.G. OZONE-POSTBOXES

- Suppose 10 SmokeStack Servers have the Ozone-Postpbox defined with the Password "Jupiter". Also suppose that they're all accessible. You have two SmokeStacks at home.

- Participant A defines Ozone "Jupiter" on Smoke Crypto Chat Messenger and connects to a public interface of a server. Two processes: share the identity and share the public keys. That is the only configuration that's required.
    - Stack A: Ozone "Jupiter".
    - Stack B: Ozone "Jupiter".
    - Stack Z: Ozone "Jupiter".
    - You: Ozone "Jupiter".
    - Friend: Ozone "Jupiter".
    - Other Friend: Ozone "Jupiter".

- Your Post Box is meant to live either in a house, in a car, in a cleaned basement, in a root, in a water-proof container, in space.

- Your friend turns off the Messenger client or has lost the connection and the user has nothing!

- A SmokeStack-Server on Android is persistent. It's a separate device. It's a discarded device.

- SmokeStack creates carbon copies. More connected SmokeStacks, more copies.

- Very simple, very elegant, very redundant, very complete, very functional.

Ackermann & Klein: Caesura in Cryptography (2020)

BRIDGING P2P WEBSEARCH: YACY & SPOT-ON

Spot-On Encryption Suite

- Spot-On URL search is a free distributed search engine, built on principles of peer-to-peer (P2P) networks and is compatible with GoldBug URL-Database.

- Its core is a computer program written in C and an inherit function within the Echo Network.

- Encrypted URL Transfer via HTTP(S).

- Encrypted URL Storage.

- RSS Feed URL import & Webcrawler Pandamonium for URL import.

- Website Storage for local browsing without Internet. Revisions for file updates of archives sites.

- Client & Web-Interface.

- Todo: Bridge to YaCy-Network.

- YaCy (pronounced "ya see") is a free distributed search engine, built on principles of peer-to-peer (P2P) networks.

- Its core is a computer program written in Java distributed on several hundred computers, so-called YaCy-peers.

- Each YaCy-peer independently crawls through the Internet, analyzes and indexes found web pages, and stores indexing results in a database (so called index) which is shared with other YaCy-peers using principles of P2P networks.

- It is a free search engine that has within the YaCy-network a decentralised architecture.

- All YaCy-peers are equal and no central server exists.

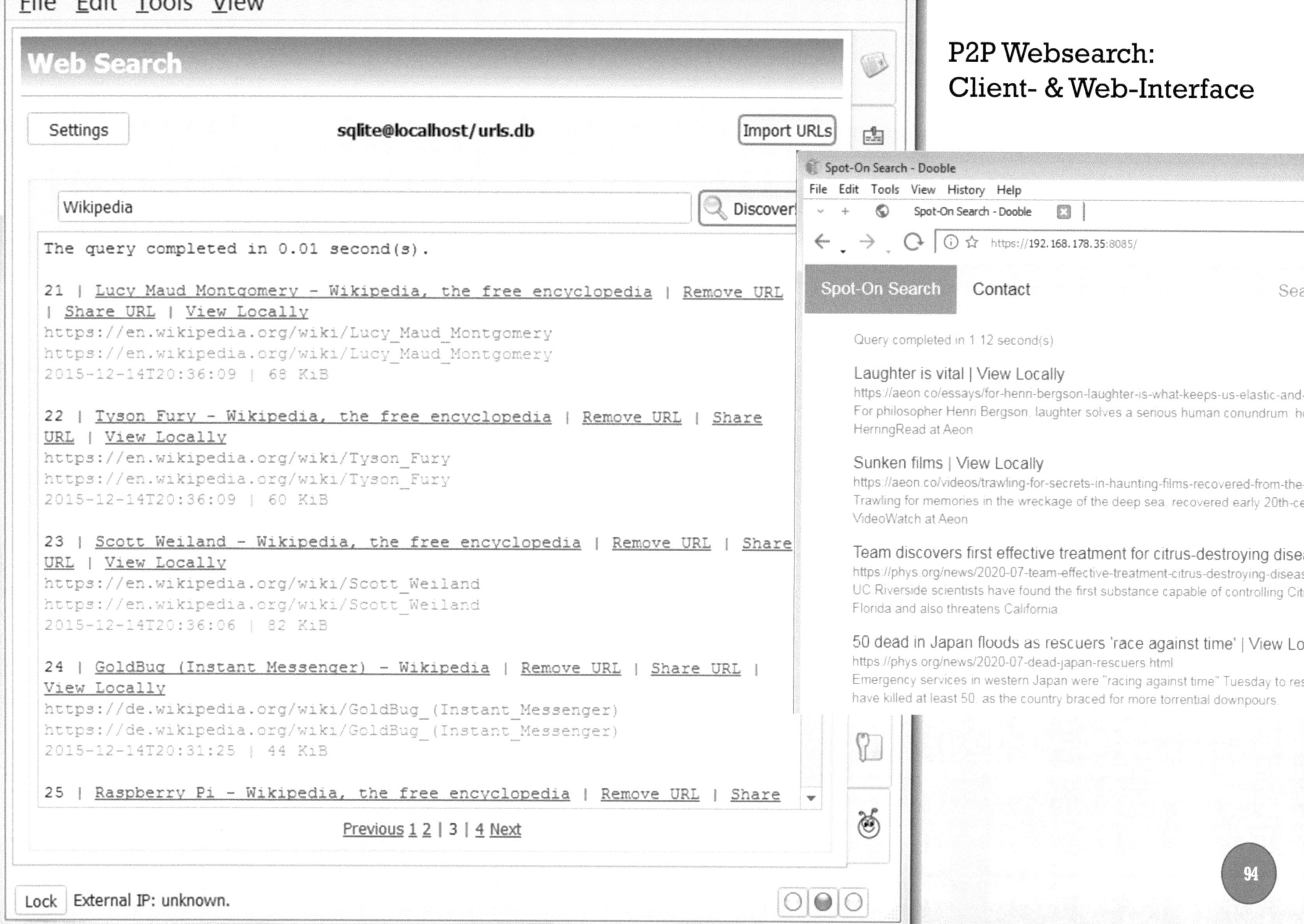

P2P Websearch:
Client- & Web-Interface

ANONYMITY ON THE INTERNET
TOR-BROWSER & ECHO-NETWORK & I2P

Spot-On
Encryption Suite

Ackermann & Klein: Caesura in Cryptography (2020)

- Tor is free and open-source software for enabling anonymous communication. The name derived from the acronym for the original software project name "The Onion Router". Tor directs Internet traffic through a free, worldwide, volunteer overlay network consisting of more than seven thousand relays to conceal a user's location and usage from anyone conducting network surveillance or traffic analysis.

- The Echo Network provides with its Clients a secure instant chat messaging and encrypting e-mailing that also include additional features such as group chat, file transfer, and a URL search based on an implemented URL data-base, which can be peer-to-peer connected to other nodes. Also some pass-through and proxy features are given. Web Proxy Exit Nodes are under development.

- The Invisible Internet Project (I2P) is an anonymous network layer (implemented as a Mix Network) that allows for censorship-resistant, peer to peer communication. Anonymous connections are achieved by encrypting the user's traffic (by using end-to-end encryption), and sending it through a volunteer-run network.

ECHO NETWORK — A KIND OF TOR?

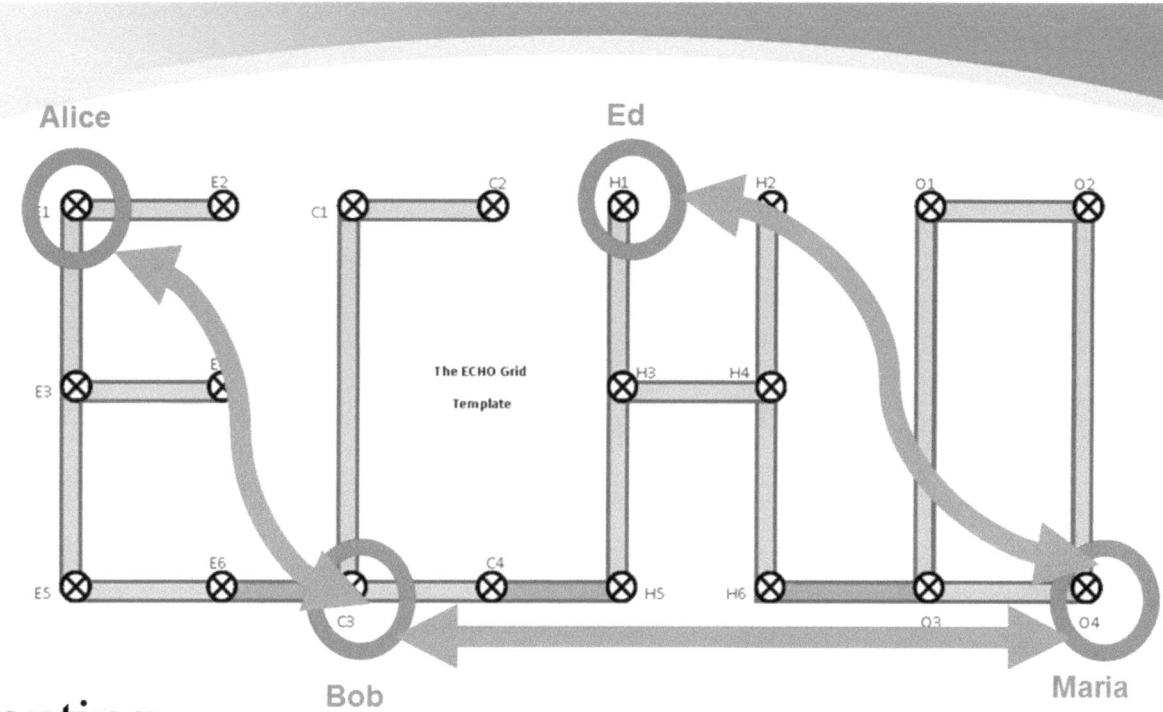

- Beyond Cryptographic Routing

- Echo Encapsulation with Multi-Encryption

- IP Addresses hidden & No Data Retention

- Exit Nodes to Web currently under development

- Adaptive Echo (AE) steers messages

- Nodes can be Server and Client

- Kind of Mesh Network

- Congestion Control

NEW RESEARCH ON
MULTIPLE CONNECTED OVERLAY NETWORKS

Idea: Connecting different Overlay-Networks like Tor, Echo, I2P, etc.

- E.g. GoldBug Client => Tor => Internet => Tor => Spot-On Client
- E.g. Gnunet => GoldBug => I2P => I2P Routing => I2P => GoldBug => Gnunet
- E.g. Echo Client => I2P => Gnunet Routing => Internet => Echo Client Spot-On
- E.g. Gnunet => I2P => I2P Routing => Tor => Gnunet
- E.g. Browser => Pass Through Echo Network => Webserver
- any other mixture…

Home > Profi IT > Sicherheit > Anonymisierungsnetzwerke

Tor, I2p, Gnunet, RetroShare, Freenet, GoldBug: Spurlos im Web

PC WELT

13.12.2014 , 17:30 Uhr , Thomas Joos

Tor, I2p, Gnunet, RetroShare, Freenet, GoldBug und Konsorten - wir stellen Anonymisierungsnetzwerke für die unterschiedlichsten Zwecke vor. Damit surfen Sie nicht nur ohne Spuren zu hinterlassen, sondern tauschen auch Dateien und chatten anonym.

MAGIC QUADRANT

- Leaders
- Challengers
- Visionaries
- Niche Players

within

Crypto Tools

Create three groups.

Please place brands like BouncyCastle, GoldBug, RetroShare, Smoke, Tor etc. with a dot into the Magic Quadrant.

Find and document criteria to judge each tool.

#TEE: TRUSTED EXECUTION ENVIRONMENT A KIOSK SYSTEM LIKE TAILS & KNOPPIX?

- Machine for Encryption is maiden and has never been connected to the internet.

- „Going the Extra Mile" (Bertram 2019): First device should be a #TEE: The encryption process needs to be done on an unmonitored machine.

- Capable Operating System without Internet: Windows 10 is regarded as an illegal operating system if not connected to the internet within the activation phase: Once the 180 days have expired, Windows 10 will randomly shut down. Switch to an open source operating system today!

- Operating system could be a KIOSK system, starting maiden after reboot and washing out all user and update data:

- No Injection into the operating system over Air, Cable or USB (compare „Stuxnet") should have been possible. This includes updates.

- Trusted Execution Environment (TEE).

- Solving the problem to transport Ciphertext from the non-net-machine to the net-machine: Spot-On Encryption Suite allows SCTP, UDF & Bluetooth connections, which are regularly „not trained for Injections" (Wake 2020).

#NNC: NON-NETWORKED CRYPTOGRAPHY TRUSTED EXECUTION ENVIRONMENTS SEPERATED

- Mancy A. Wake founding the Non-Networked Cryptography in the Internet age.

- Offline Cryptography has always been there.

- Non-Networked Cryptography takes place on a seperated secure embedded system (SEES).

- „Echo on a Chip" shows a reference model for EoC #1.

- Replacing TCP with other protocols, temporarily connected like Bluetooth.

- Solving the transport problem with queiing and packets to be shifted from trusted platform to connected and networked platform.

ISBN 9783751916448

Ackermann & Klein: Caesura in Cryptography (2020)

SECURE ARCHITECTURE MODEL (SAM) EXTENDS THE OSI-LAYER MODEL

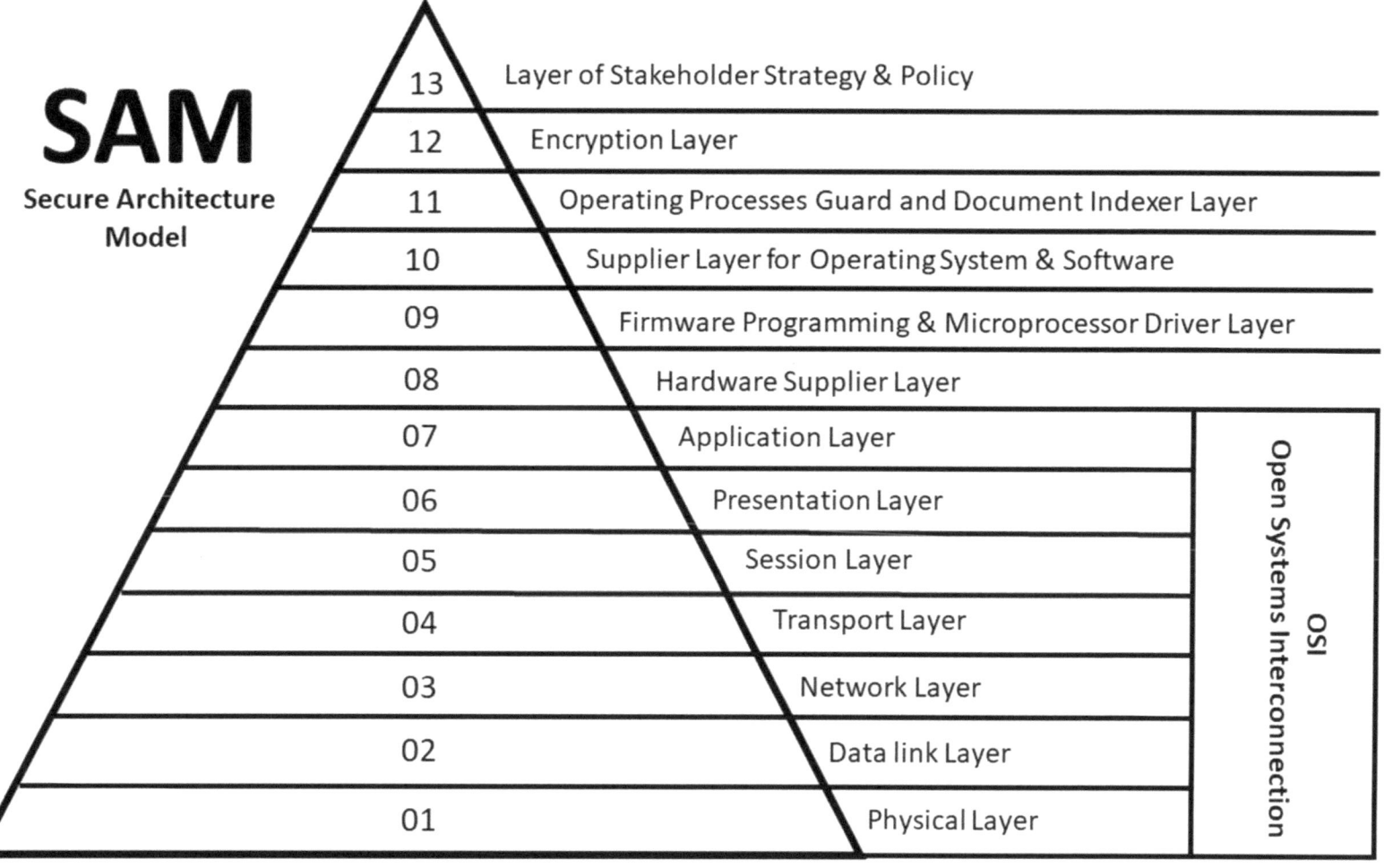

SAM

Secure Architecture Model

13	Layer of Stakeholder Strategy & Policy
12	Encryption Layer
11	Operating Processes Guard and Document Indexer Layer
10	Supplier Layer for Operating System & Software
09	Firmware Programming & Microprocessor Driver Layer
08	Hardware Supplier Layer
07	Application Layer
06	Presentation Layer
05	Session Layer
04	Transport Layer
03	Network Layer
02	Data link Layer
01	Physical Layer

OSI
Open Systems Interconnection

Source: Wake, Mancy A. / Hibernack, Dorothy / Lullaby, Lucas (2020): Echo on a Chip - A New Perception for the Next Generation of Micro-Controllers handling Encryption for Mobile Messaging: From Secure Embedded Systems to Separated Secure Embedded Systems (SSES) in Cryptography, p. 87, Norderstedt, ISBN 9783751916448.

PODIUM DISCUSSION (FISH BOWL EXERCISE): TOOLS VERSUS POLICY?

- A fishbowl conversation is a form of dialog that can be used when discussing topics within large groups. Fishbowl conversations are sometimes also used in participatory events such as unconferences. The advantage of fishbowl is that it allows the entire group to participate in a conversation. Several people can join the discussion.

Discuss, if security is created by

- installing and providing training in software tools

- or by providing (or speaking against) crypto policies.

- Find arguments based on historical reports

  on so called „crypto dialogues". What is that?

CRYPTO WARS: USA STEERS MORE THAN ONE THIRD OF THE CRYPTO MARKET. IN GERMANY & FRANCE EVERY **SECOND** CRYPTO TOOL IS FREE & OPEN SOURCE.

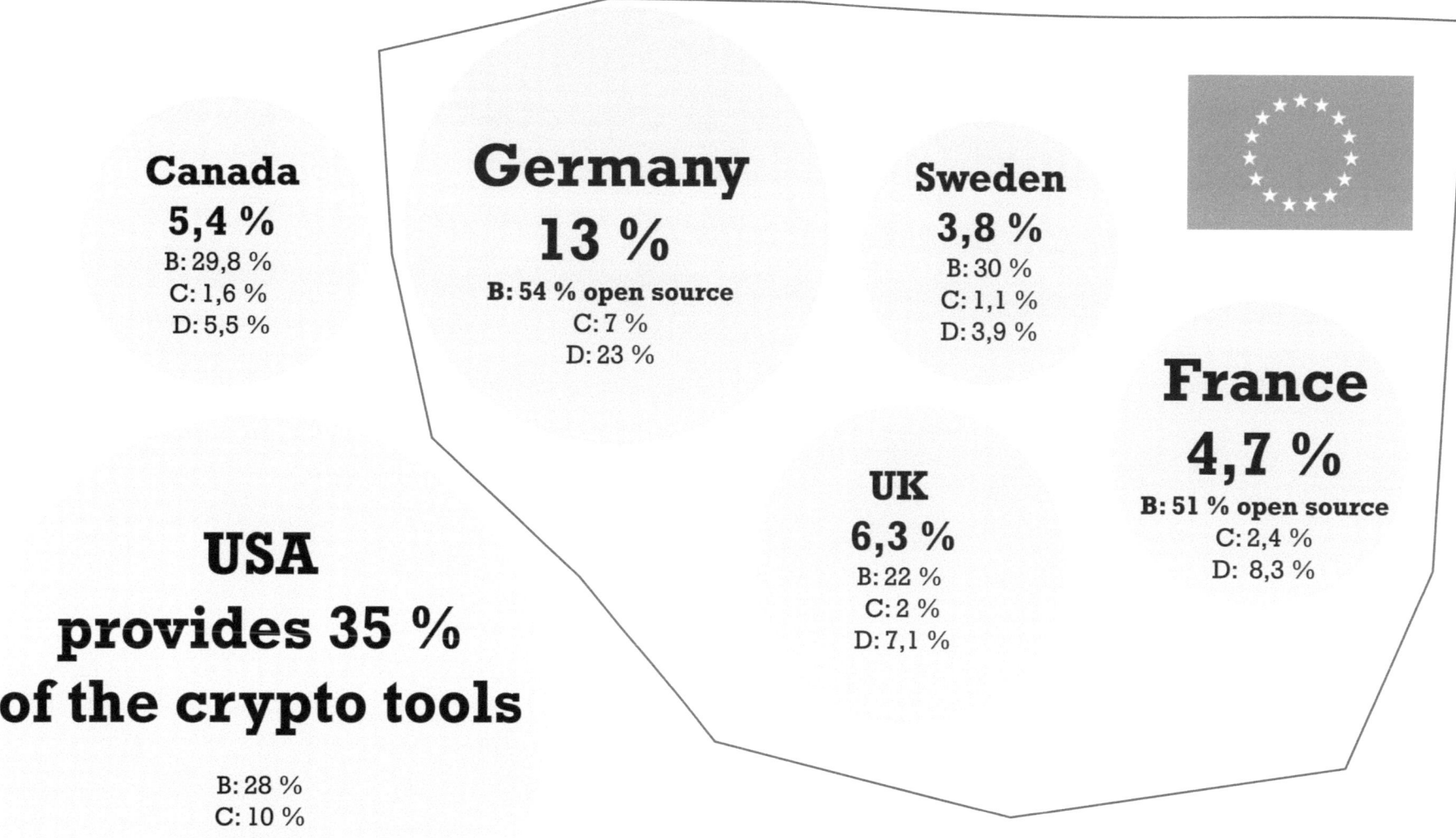

Canada
5,4 %
B: 29,8 %
C: 1,6 %
D: 5,5 %

Germany
13 %
B: 54 % open source
C: 7 %
D: 23 %

Sweden
3,8 %
B: 30 %
C: 1,1 %
D: 3,9 %

France
4,7 %
B: 51 % open source
C: 2,4 %
D: 8,3 %

UK
6,3 %
B: 22 %
C: 2 %
D: 7,1 %

USA
provides 35 %
of the crypto tools
B: 28 %
C: 10 %
D: 34 %

A: % Marketshare within worldwide available crypto tools/projects (N=865).
B: % of these tools from this country are free & open source (N=ref. nat. projects).
C: % of the worldwide tools are open source tools from this country (N=865).
D: % of all open source crypto tools worldwide are from this country (N=254).

Ackermann & Klein: Caesura in Cryptography (2020)

N = 254 free & open source crypto tools of 865 crypto tool in total, surveyed within 2016 by Schneier et al. / own calculations.

SOUVEREIGNITY: ESTABLISHMENT OF OWN NATIONAL CRYPTO PROJECTS

- Open source leaders in cryptographic projects are those who are also a market leader in cryptographic projects.

- **Over 254 open source tools & active projects** in 2016: to be recounted and refreshed per country for the future.

- 1/3 of encryption projects deal with communication.

- Message Encryption is more vivid than Mail Encryption.

- POPTASTIC & Delta Chat has **harmonized encrypted Mail & Messaging** since 2016.

- If national tools are open source, they are for a worldwide use. Then also server infrastrucure has to be considered for a national souvereignity (e.g. for Messaging).

- **Your contribution for open source cryptography matters!**

CATEGORY	USA	GERMANY	FRANCE	UK	CANADA	SWEDEN
OPEN SOURCE CYPTO TOOLS	87	60	21	18	14	10
TOTAL CRYPTO TOOLS	304	112	41	54	47	33
MESSAGE ENCRYPTION PROJECTS	86	15	8	14	12	2
MAIL ENCRYPTION PROJECTS	19	16	6	2	9	3
MAIL & MESSAGE TOOLS IN TOTAL	105	31	14	16	21	5

EXAMPLES OF NATIONAL LIGHTHOUSE PROJECTS

- Australia # BouncyCastle # http://bouncycastle.org
- Austria # GoldBug Chat Messenger # http://goldbug.sf.net
- Canada # BigBlueButton # https://bigbluebutton.org/
- Canada # LibreSSL # http://libressl.org
- Finland # Dooble Web Browser # http://dooble.sourceforge.net
- France # Retroshare # http://retroshare.sf.net/
- France # VeraCrypt # http://veracrypt.codeplex.com
- Germany # GnuPG – libgcrypt # http://gnupg.org
- India # BitCHat # https://mesh.im/
- Israel # Viber # http://viber.com
- Italy # Kontalk # http://kontalk.org
- Japan # Sylpheed # http://sylpheed.sraoss.jp/en
- Netherlands # Pastebin # http://pastebin.com
- Russia # DiskCryptor # http://diskcryptor.net
- Sweden # Open SSH # http://openssh.com
- Switzerland # PEP (Pretty Easy Privacy) # http://pep-project.org
- United Kingdom # Briar # http://briarproject.org
- United States # Jitsi # http://jitsi.org
- United States # Mumble # http://wiki.mumble.info/wiki/Main_Page
- United States # Signal # http://whispersystems.org
- United States # Smoke Crypto Chat # https://textbrowser.github.io/smoke/
- United States # Spot-On Encryption Suite # https://spot-on.sf.net
- United States # Tor Browser # http://torproject.org

The **Five Eyes (FVEY)** is an intelligence alliance comprising Australia, Canada, New Zealand, the United Kingdom and the United States. These countries are parties to the multilateral UKUSA Agreement, a treaty for joint cooperation in signals intelligence.

Ackermann & Klein: Caesura in Cryptography (2020)

Based on Schneier at al. 2016

WE WANT YOU

IN A CRYPTOGRAPHIC PROJECT

.. either in an open source project for your nation and the world community,
.. either providing cryptographic infrastructure within your country,
.. or keeping up the cryptographic learning, thinking, resarch and culture,
.. and running science & business
      based on consulting, teaching, developing and maintainance.

POPULAR QUOTATIONS:
„ENCRYPTION IS LIKE MATHS FOR EVERYBODY"

- *"The reality is, if you put a back door in, that back door is for everybody, for good guys and bad guys."* - **Tim Cook, CEO Apple**, https://www.independent.co.uk/life-style/gadgets-and-tech/news/tim-cook-apple-privacy-encryption-a6781441.html

- *"We think encryption is a must in today's world. No-one should have to decide privacy or security. We should be smart enough to have both."* - **Tim Cook, CEO Apple,** https://www.independent.co.uk/life-style/gadgets-and-tech/news/tim-cook-apple-privacy-encryption-a6781441.html

- *"The question is not 'do you have something to hide?' - The question is whether we control or they controls us."* - **Oliver Stone, Filmmaker,** http://www.youtube.com/watch?v=0U37hl0n9mY

- *Why Apple wants to encrypt end-to-end: "We don't feel like we should be in the middle of [messaging]. I'm the FedEx guy. I'm taking your package and I'm delivering it. I just do it like this. My job isn't to open it up, make a copy of it, put it over in my cabinet in case somebody later wants to come say, I'd like to see your messages. That's not a role that I play. It's not a role that I think I should play. And it's certainly not a role I think you want me to play."* - **Tim Cook, CEO Apple,** https://www.cultofmac.com/418213/tim-cook-encryption-interview/

- *"Back doors are a gift to Desperados"* - **Facebook, Jay Sullivan** https://www.nzz.ch/international/verschluesselung-facebook-apple-ld.1528273

- *"The unconditional restriction of human rights for everyone to protect a few is unconstitutional. In order to ensure the integrity of people, cameras should be abolished and not encryption. The expansion of data retention and restriction on data encryption does not help against cybercrime any more than the reduction of streets to protect against bank break-ins."* **Prof. Dr. Jan Onderwater,** https://www.heise.de/forum-454588/

- *"People in top positions have `no idea´ what they are talking about: In general, I see governments not understanding technology very well. Referring to officials attempting to ban end-to-end encryption - a secret way of communicating in which eavesdroppers cannot access messages - I likened it to attempting to ban mathematics. The software is there, and shared online. You can't ban it."* - **Jimmy Wales, CEO Wikipedia,** https://news.sky.com/story/wiki-boss-encryption-ban-like-banning-maths-10343807

EVALUATION OF THIS COURSE

Please check for each topic & chapter your content & learning profile.

	♡ This is what I liked. ☑	☺ This was new to me. ☑	⬇ Here I want deeper research provided. ☑
▪ Algorithm			
▪ Apps			
▪ Bibliography			
▪ Challengers			
▪ Compared to			
▪ Exercise			
▪ Friends			
▪ Interest in			
▪ Library			
▪ Protocols			
▪ Proud of			
▪ Quotation			
▪ Servers			
▪ Tools			
▪ Vision			

TIPPS TO CREATE YOUR OWN SLIDES

- Use not the same layout and ductus in each slide

- Try to focus on different views on Cryptography (customers, beginners, students, developers etc.).

- Keep the Helicopter perspective: Dont explain all AES rounds in detail, as this is worth an own book! – max 2 slides per cryptographic issue.

- Not more than a few sentences on one slide.

- Keep in mind you need 3 minutes per slide to talk about, 30 minutes presentation and 30 minutes questions need only 10 slides per lesson!

- Provide literature references on the backup slides.

- Be up to date and don't show the old tirades of all others! (though many made their career based on repetition of old stati!)

- Ask your teacher to update her/his slides!

- Dont tell your audience the beginning with Adam and Eva – they are dead. So is DES, Curve ECDSA and RSA.

- Provide a vision of tomorrow and a motivation for learning.

LITERATURE & BIBLIOGRAPHY

This "Encyclopedia of modern Cryptography and Internet Security" brings the latest and most relevant coverage of the topic - expanding a lot of relevant terms and central key words: *It's a Nomenclatura!*

- Fundamental information on modern Cryptography and Internet Security in a broadband overview.
- Extensive resource with most relevant explanations of keywords and terms.
- Introduction article by editing authors on "Transformation of Cryptography".
- Effective handbook for students, tutors and researching professionals in many fields

This modern Encyclopedia is broad in scope, covering everything from AutoCrypt and Exponential Encryption to Zero-Knowledge-Proof Keys including explanations on Authentication, Block Ciphers and Stream Ciphers, Cryptanalysis and Security, Cryptographic Calling and Cryptographic Discovery, Cryptographic Protocols like e.g. the Echo-Protocol, Elliptic Curve Cryptography, Fiasco Forwarding, Goldbugs, Hash Functions and MACs, Juggling Juggernauts and Juggerknot Keys, McEliece, Multi-Encryption, NTRU, OTM, Public Key Cryptography, Patch-Points, POPTASTIC, Quantum Computing Cryptography, Secret Streams, Turtle Hopping, Two-Way-Calling and many more...

Nomenclatura - Encyclopedia of modern Cryptography and Internet Security: From AutoCrypt and Exponential Encryption to Zero-Knowledge-Proof Keys. ISBN: 978-3748191513 & ISBN: 978-3746066684.

LITERATURE & BIBLIOGRAPHY

- Adams, David / Maier, Ann-Kathrin (2016): BIG SEVEN Study, open source crypto messengers to be compared - or: Comprehensive Confidentiality Review & Audit of GoldBug, Encrypting E-Mail-Client & Secure Instant Messenger, Descriptions, tests and analysis reviews of 20 functions of the application GoldBug based on the essential fields and methods of evaluation of the 8 major international audit manuals for IT security investigations including 38 figures and 87 tables, English / German Language, 305 pages, June 2016, ISBN 9783750408975.

- Arute, Frank / Martinis, John M. & et al. (2019): Quantum supremacy using a programmable superconducting processor, Nature volume 574, pages505–510 (23. October 2019)

- Bertram, Linda A. / van Dooble, Gunther: Transformation of Cryptography, 2019, ISBN: 978-3749450749.

- Filby, P.W. (1995): Floradora and a Unique Break into One-Time Pad ciphers. Journal of Intelligence and National Security, 10:3, p. 408–422, doi:10.1080/02684529508432310.

- Gasakis, Mele / Schmidt, Max: Beyond Cryptographic Routing: The Echo Protocol in the new Era of Exponential Encryption (EEE), 2018, ISBN: 978-3748151982.

- Hahn, Tobias / Herfert, Michael / Lange, Benjamin (2015): Pro Privacy, URL https://www.sit.fraunhofer.de/fileadmin/dokumente/studien_und_technical_reports/Abschlussbericht-Pro-Privacy.pdf

- McEliece, Robert J. (1978): A Public-Key Cryptosystem Based On Algebraic Coding Theory, DSN Progress Report. 44: 114-116.

- McNoodle Library (2016): Implementation of the McEliece Algorithm in C++, GitHub.

- NIST (2016) / Chen, Lily / Jordan, Stephen / Liu, Yi-Kai / Moody, Dustin / Peralta, Rene / Perlner, Ray / Smith-Tone, Daniel: NISTIR 8105, DRAFT, Report on Post-Quantum Cryptography, URL: http://csrc.nist.gov/publications/drafts/nistir-8105/nistir_8105_draft.pdf, National Institute of Standards and Technology. February 2016.

- Nomenclatura - Encyclopedia of modern Cryptography and Internet Security, ISBN: 978-3748191513 & ISBN: 978-3746066684.

- Pednault, Edwin / Gunnels, John A. / Nannicini, Giacomo / Horesh, Lior / Wisnieff, Robert: Summit supercomputer at Oak Ridge National Laboratories - Leveraging Secondary Storage to Simulate Deep 54-qubit Sycamore Circuits, IBM T.J. Watson Research Center, NY, URL: https://arxiv.org/pdf/1910.09534.pdf

- Popescu, Bogdan C. / Crispo, Bruno / Tanenbaum, Andrew S. (2004): Safe and Private Data Sharing with Turtle: Friends Team-Up and Beat the System, http://turtle-p2p.sourceforge.net/documents.html

- Quisquater, Jean-Jacques / Guillou, Louis C. / Berson, Thomas A. (1990): How to Explain Zero-Knowledge Protocols to Your Children, Advances in Cryptology – CRYPTO '89, 435, pp. 628–631.

- Rieffel, Eleanor G. / NASA/TP-2019-220319 (2019): Quantum Supremacy Using a Programmable Superconducting Processor, NASA Ames Research Center, National Aeronautics and Space Administration, Ames Research Center, Moffett Field, URL: https://www.inverse.com/article/59507-full-quantum-supremacy-paper, California, August.

- Ritter, Terry (1995): Ritter's Crypto Glossary and Dictionary of Technical Cryptography, Comments on Multi-Encryption, URL: http://www.ciphersbyritter.com/GLOSSARY.HTM#MultipleEncryption

- Schneier, Bruce / Seidel, Kathleen / Vijayakumar, Saranya: A Worldwide Survey of Encryption Products, URL: https://www.schneier.com/academic/paperfiles/worldwide-survey-of-encryption-products.pdf, February 11, 2016 Version 1.0.

- Spot-On Encryption Suite: Democratization of Multiple & Exponential Encryption: - Handbook and User Manual as practical software guide, ISBN: 978-3749435067.

- Wake, Mancy et al. (2020): Echo on a Chip (EoC) - A New Perception for the Next Generation of Micro-controllers handling Encryption for Mobile Messaging: From Secure Embedded Systems to Separated Secure Embedded Systems (SSES) in Cryptography, Hardware supported Trusted Execution Environments (TEE), ISBN: 9783751916448.